T0275278

A PHILOSOPHER LOOKS AT DIGITAL COMMUNICATION

Communication is complicated, and so is the ethics of communication. We communicate about innumerable topics, to varied audiences, using a gamut of technologies. The ethics of communication, therefore, has to address a wide range of technical, ethical and epistemic requirements. In this book, Onora O'Neill shows how digital technologies have made communication more demanding: they can support communication with huge numbers of distant and dispersed recipients; they can amplify or suppress selected content; and they can target or ignore selected audiences. Often this is done anonymously, making it harder for readers and listeners, viewers and browsers, to assess which claims are true or false, reliable or misleading, flaky or fake. So how can we empower users to assess and evaluate digital communication, so that they can tell which standards it meets and which it flouts? That is the challenge which this book explores.

ONORA O'NEILL is Honorary Professor Emeritus at the University of Cambridge and a crossbench member of the House of Lords. She is the author of numerous books on Kant, ethics and political philosophy, including *Justice Across Boundaries* (Cambridge University Press, 2016).

A Philosopher Looks at

In this series, philosophers offer a personal and philosophical exploration of a topic of general interest.

Books in the series

Raymond Geuss, *A Philosopher Looks at Work*
Paul Guyer, *A Philosopher Looks at Architecture*
Stephen Mumford, *A Philosopher Looks at Sport*
Onora O'Neill, *A Philosopher Looks at Digital Communication*
Michael Ruse, *A Philosopher Looks at Human Beings*

A PHILOSOPHER LOOKS AT

DIGITAL
COMMUNICATION

ONORA O'NEILL

CAMBRIDGE
UNIVERSITY PRESS

CAMBRIDGE
UNIVERSITY PRESS

University Printing House, Cambridge CB2 8BS, United Kingdom

One Liberty Plaza, 20th Floor, New York, NY 10006, USA

477 Williamstown Road, Port Melbourne, VIC 3207, Australia

314–321, 3rd Floor, Plot 3, Splendor Forum, Jasola District Centre,
New Delhi – 110025, India

103 Penang Road, #05-06/07, Visioncrest Commercial, Singapore 238467

Cambridge University Press is part of the University of Cambridge.

It furthers the University's mission by disseminating knowledge in the pursuit of
education, learning, and research at the highest international levels of excellence.

www.cambridge.org
Information on this title: www.cambridge.org/9781108986816
DOI: 10.1017/9781108981583

First published 2022

Printed in the United Kingdom by TJ Books Limited, Padstow Cornwall

A catalogue record for this publication is available from the British Library.

Library of Congress Cataloging-in-Publication Data
NAMES: O'Neill, Onora, 1941– author.
TITLE: A philosopher looks at digital communication / Onora O'Neill.
DESCRIPTION: Cambridge, United Kingdom ; New York, NY, USA : Cambridge
  University Press, 2021. | Series: A philosopher looks at | Includes bibliographical
  references and index.
IDENTIFIERS: LCCN 2021035337 (print) | LCCN 2021035338 (ebook) | ISBN 9781108986816
  (paperback) | ISBN 9781108981583 (epub)
SUBJECTS: LCSH: Internet–Moral and ethical aspects. | Telecommunication–
  Philosophy. | Telecommunication–Social aspects. | BISAC: PHILOSOPHY / Ethics &
  Moral Philosophy
CLASSIFICATION: LCC TK5105.878 .O54 2021 (print) | LCC TK5105.878 (ebook) |
  DDC 175–dc23
LC record available at https://lccn.loc.gov/2021035337
LC ebook record available at https://lccn.loc.gov/2021035338

ISBN 978-1-108-98681-6 Paperback

CONTENTS

Preface   *page* xi

Part I Complex Communication   1

1   Presuppositions of Communication   3
    Accessibility, Intelligibility and Assessability   3
    Widening Accessibility: Spreading the Word   5
    Some Limits of Digital Communication   8
    The Wider Context   11

2   Acts and Content, Norms and Harms   15
    Speech Acts and Speech Content   15
    Norms or Harms?   17
    Private Harms   19
    Public Harms   21
    Norms and Standards for Communicating   24

3   Communication and New Technologies   28
    Norms and Practical Judgement   28
    Ancient Norms for Communication   32
    Socrates' Warning   34
    Readers, Listeners and Viewers   37
    Traditional Intermediaries   41

4   Digital Hopes   44
    The Promise of Connectivity   44
    'Breaking' the Intermediaries   47

vii

Misgivings and Criticisms   51
Intermediaries and Democracy   53

Part II Norms and Standards in a Connected World   59

5   Duties and Rights 1: Freedom of Expression   61
Rights Before Duties: Historical Sketch   61
The Turn to Rights: Freedom of Expression   64
Communication or Expression?   67
Circumstances Alter Cases   68
Private and Public Harms   71

6   Duties and Rights 2: Rights to Privacy   75
Privacy Overview   75
The Point of Privacy   78
Data Protection and 'Personal Information'   80
Personal and Sensitive Information   82
Informed Consent and Personal Data   84
Privacy in Practice   86

Part III Politics and Connectivity   89

7   Power and Anonymity   91
A Turning Point?   91
A Profusion of Proposals   94
Accountable Communication and Anonymity   96
States and Corporations, Customers and Users   99
Anonymity and Privacy   104
Anonymity and Democracy   106
Intermediaries Again: Old and New   108
Platforms and Publishers   110
Limiting Anonymity, Extending Accountability   113

CONTENTS

Notes   115
Some Suggestions for Further Reading   129
Index   132

PREFACE

The ethics of communication is distinctive because communication includes a huge, complex and diverse range of activities that penetrate and shape every part of human life. All communication requires at least two parties – an originator and a recipient, or multiple originators and recipients – who must have specific and linkable capacities to satisfy and to recognise the many technical, ethical and epistemic standards that bear on communication.

To communicate successfully, recipients must be *accessible* to originators (while two-way communication requires two-way accessibility); they must share an *intelligible* language; and they must see communication as open to *assessment* or *interpretation* of various types. Intelligibility, accessibility and assessability are needed for all communication, whether or not it is either ethically or epistemically adequate. They are needed not only for honest and accurate communication, but also for deceptive and manipulative communication. They are prerequisites for routine shopping and effective business transactions, for daily chatter and technical exchanges, but also for misleading claims and defamatory accusations, and for endless varieties of deception and fraud, including propaganda and disinformation campaigning.

Digital technologies have transformed communication across the last thirty or more years. There are vast and sprawling literatures on these transformations, and on the advantages and problems produced by specific uses of digital technologies. A lot of discussions focus on specific technologies, or uses of technologies, and the benefits and problems to which they give rise. However, rather less has been written about the bearing of long-standing accounts of the ethics of communication on digital communication. That is what I shall explore in this short book.

The most obvious, and the most important, change is that digital technologies have transformed accessibility by providing hugely expanded connectivity. This expansion has produced both amazing benefits and serious difficulties. It enables almost instantaneous communication across the globe, yet can leave recipients unable to identify the provenance or assess the credentials of the communication they receive, and leaves originators unsure whom their recipients include.

At first many claimed optimistically that greater connectivity would support, or even ensure, more and better communication, and that this would benefit many activities, and in particular public life and democratic politics. The actual results have been mixed. Ramifying connectivity allows wider communication. But in practice it may leave recipients less able to identify originators, and originators less sure whom their audiences include. This can make it harder for recipients to assess whether what is communicated is reliable or adequately evidenced, ethically acceptable or unacceptable. When provenance is unclear or hidden, it can be hard to tell whether the content communicated is true or false, honest or dishonest, reliable or flaky. Digital communication can also make it harder for originators to tell whom their communication will reach, fuelling doubts about privacy and other aspects of communication. Increased connectivity indeed supports *wider* communication, but does not always secure *better* communication that meets important ethical and epistemic norms and standards.

This could, perhaps, have been foreseen. This is not the first time that communication has been seriously disrupted by technological change. Earlier innovations in communication technologies – among them writing, printing and broadcasting – all led to problems. Many of these were resolved by changes in the organisation and cultures of communication. The ways in which the difficulties arising from past innovations were addressed may offer clues for dealing with some of the disruptions and challenges that digital technologies are currently raising for online communication.

It is clear enough that the issues raised by digital communication are complicated. Many contemporary discussions of the ethical issues, and particularly of those that matter for communicating with wider audiences, including for democratic politics, take strikingly narrow views of the ethical and epistemic standards that matter for communication. Some approaches focus largely on requirements to respect human rights, so give great weight to the two human rights that mainly bear on communication: freedom of expression and rights to privacy. These are indeed important ethical requirements, and I shall discuss them.[1] But many other familiar norms and standards for communication – including some that have been taken seriously for centuries, and a few that have mattered for millennia – are now quite often treated as matters that can be trumped by requirements to protect freedom of expression and privacy, and are taken seriously only if mandated by specific legal or institutional requirements.

In effect, we now find ourselves inhabiting a digital world in which connectivity has widened the channels and the range of communication, yet often relying on a narrower range of ethical standards than used to be taken seriously, and assuming that they will be sufficient for the ethics of digital communication. This discrepancy is, I think, one reason why discussion of the ethics of digital communication has become difficult, fragmented and controversial. It may also offer clues to some ways in which problems might be addressed and reduced.

I shall not, however, discuss or endorse detailed proposals for legal and regulatory change, or try to describe or assess the merits and deficiencies of the many complex proposals currently under discussion in many jurisdictions. Doing so would require an enormously long book on the feasibility and effectiveness of complex ranges of legal and regulatory measures in and across many jurisdictions, and would date rapidly. This book is about the ethics, not the regulation, of digital communication, so I shall first try to get a handle on some of the underlying sources of ethical problems. If that proves feasible, it may bear on formulating, selecting and discarding proposals for legal and regulatory reform.

So, I shall comment on technical, ethical and epistemic standards and norms that matter for ethically acceptable and epistemically robust communication, including digital communication. I shall stress the importance of taking account of a wide range of norms and standards, and bringing them to bear on the distinctive ways in which digital technologies can be used to shape communication. Formulating an adequate approach to the ethics of digital communication and identifying effective ways of securing the range of relevant ethical and epistemic standards will not be easy, but it may be possible to identify some of the steps that are needed.

Part I

Complex Communication

1   Presuppositions of Communication

Accessibility, Intelligibility and Assessability

Communication includes a wide and distinctive range of activities that link originators to recipients. Like other complex activities, it must meet both technical standards and ethical and epistemic norms. Unsurprisingly discussion of many of the norms and standards that bear on communication is an age-old theme. And unsurprisingly these norms and standards may need review and reconsideration if we are to reach a convincing view of the ethics of communication that uses new technologies.

Many of the technical standards for communicating successfully are highly specific. They depend on the aims of those who seek to communicate, the symbolic systems and technologies they use, and the audiences they seek to reach. However, all communication must meet three generic technical requirements if it is to succeed. What originators seek to communicate must be *accessible* to recipient(s), must be *intelligible* to them, and must be *assessable* by them in ways that support understanding and interpretation, and enable forms of check and challenge. These three very broad technical requirements bear on all communication. Each is needed for communication to succeed, whether it is ethically acceptable or unacceptable, whether it is epistemically robust or flaky.

Accessibility can be secured in many ways. Originators and recipients are sometimes immediately present to one another, with direct access to and awareness of one another's communication. In other cases, they may be physically distant from one another, but linked in ways that enable communication. Sometimes these links are provided by chains of individual intermediaries, each with access to at least one other. In other cases, originator and recipient may be part of a network of interconnected communicators, or of a public sphere in which communication can travel by many routes and reach varied audiences. And in many cases, accessibility is supported by technologies, including writing and printing, broadcasting and film, as well as digital technologies.

Intelligibility requires originators and recipients to share (at least) elements of a common language or other symbolic system, which may use speech, or written symbols, images or music. Shared natural languages are typically supported by complex cultural practices and standards, often reinforced by mutually intelligible facial expressions and gestures, by illustrations, sounds and symbols, by conventions and courtesies. Verbal communication can be augmented – and sometimes replaced – by welcoming smiles or menacing fists, by traffic signs or familiar trademarks, by displays of sacred emblems or noisy fanfares, and by countless other forms of non-verbal communication.

Assessability is needed if recipients are to attend to, interpret or challenge others' assertions and proposals. Some aspects of assessability provide humdrum ways of checking what was communicated. Others are more ambitious and searching. They include processes and standards for interpreting or reinterpreting others' speech acts, thereby shaping or reshaping how their communication is understood, the responses it is likely to receive, and the cultural and ethical significance it will be given. Recipients are not merely passive when they attend to and grasp what others seek to communicate: they must pay attention, assimilate, assess, interpret and in some cases empathise with one another's communication. This is true of everyday conversation, of communication that uses what are occasionally (rather disparagingly) called 'legacy media' – print, radio and television – and of communication that uses digital technologies. Communication is always at least a two-way activity, and recipients too are agents.

Widening Accessibility: Spreading the Word

The accessibility of communication can be expanded in many ways. Perhaps the oldest way of making communication more widely accessible is by languages becoming more widely intelligible or translatable. Expanded intelligibility made some natural languages – Greek in the ancient Mediterranean, English in the modern world – more widely accessible as they became intelligible to more people, who could then understand and use them. In such cases, expanded accessibility piggy-backs on expanded intelligibility. However, in a world in which the number of living languages has long been falling, while human populations have been increasing, expanding the accessibility of others' communication has not generally relied on widening its intelligibility. This slow, organic way of widening accessibility has its limits, and most ways of increasing accessibility neither require nor presuppose changes in the intelligibility of specific ways of communicating.

The most obvious and the oldest way of extending accessibility without extending intelligibility is by relying on others to spread the word. Accessibility can be secured and extended by chains of human intermediaries who pass messages from speaker to speaker, from hand to hand, from rider to rider. Supporting accessibility by chains of human intermediaries has a long but chequered history. Chains are only as strong as their weakest links, and the accessibility they provide can be limited and vulnerable. In his book on testimony, the Australian philosopher Tony Coady illustrated this point with a (no doubt apocryphal) story about a wartime message that travels from the front line to headquarters by whispers passed from soldier to soldier. The original message was urgent: 'Send reinforcements, we are going to advance!'; but what arrived was less so – 'Send three-and-fourpence, we are going to a dance!'[1] As chains of intermediaries lengthen, opportunities for messages to be corrupted or lost multiply.

Other ways of extending accessibility are both more robust and more convenient than passing messages serially via successive individual communicators. The history of communication technologies is in part one of expanding accessibility by using technological rather than human intermediaries in order to reach more, or more distant, or different recipients. It is a long and complex history and includes the invention and spread of writing, of printing, of telegraphy and telephony, of broadcasting, film and television, as well as the digital revolution of the late twentieth century. Each new technology extended and reshaped accessibility in distinctive ways. Changes in accessibility in turn reshaped the ways in which recipients could understand and assess one another's communication.

Digital technologies have extended accessibility in dramatic ways, producing both changes that are welcome and beneficial, and changes that can be used to harm and wrong others. The ramifying connectivity they provide can make it harder for recipients and originators to identify one another. Where originators can be hidden from recipients, let alone when provenance is deliberately hidden or falsified, even content that is both accessible and readily intelligible may be unassessable, or less assessable, for many recipients. Conversely, when recipients can be hidden from originators, they cannot identify their audiences and may be unsure whether to communicate or what they can securely share. It is hardly surprising that conspiracy theories are flourishing in the era of digital communication technologies: no earlier communication technology has made available such rich opportunities to disrupt assessability by redirecting or controlling, targeting or suppressing, both what is communicated, and information about its originators and recipients.[2]

Digital technologies are, of course, not the first technical innovations to alter communication, nor the first to expand connectivity. Nor are they the first to disrupt established ways of communicating. New technologies have repeatedly changed ways in which originators reach recipients, the range of recipients they can reach, the ways in which communication can succeed or fail, and the extent to which recipients can follow and assess others' communication. Past accounts of problems produced by new communication technologies, and of ways in which those problems were addressed, are therefore likely to be instructive. I shall comment briefly on some of the problems that have arisen when established ways of communicating were disrupted by past technological changes, and on some ways in which disruptions were addressed.[3] Past difficulties and their resolution may shed light on some of the ethical issues that arise in using digital technologies to communicate.

Some Limits of Digital Communication

This book is specifically about the ethics of digital *communication*, so will not address the many ethical issues that arise when digital technologies are used for other purposes. So, I shall not try to cover the full range of issues sometimes labelled 'digital ethics' or 'data ethics', or to address all the ethical and epistemic issues that digital technologies have raised.

The phrases 'digital ethics' and 'data ethics' suggest, I think misleadingly, that all activities that use digital technologies raise a common set of ethical issues. Yet it is common for a technology or tool to be used for various purposes or activities that raise distinct ranges of ethical issues. For example, tables are an immensely useful technical invention: they provide flat horizontal surfaces at a convenient height for human purposes, such as eating meals and organising paperwork. But it does not follow that 'table ethics' would form a coherent or unitary inquiry. We can discuss table manners and hospitality, or office organisation and processes, and both will no doubt raise ethical (and other) issues. But it makes little sense to see all ethical questions that bear on activities that typically use tables as parts of some unitary body of thought that should be known as 'table ethics'. Ethical standards are relevant to types of *action*, and different activities that use the same tools or technologies may raise quite different issues.

I shall focus specifically on ethical issues that arise from using digital technologies *to communicate with others*, and will not cover those raised by other uses of those technologies. I shall not discuss ethical issues that can arise in designing software, or developing its applications or choosing algorithms for particular purposes, or those raised by Artificial Intelligence, machine learning, the Internet of things, robots, 'autonomous' vehicles or 'autonomous' weapons.

Nor will I cover the use of technical measures to pre-empt normative – legal, ethical, and epistemic – questions. Roger Brownsword has pointed out that 'the direction of regulatory travel is towards technological management', and argues that technical measures can block the very possibility of 'non-compliance' and preclude ethical and other normative issues.[4] When communication with human audiences is subjected to technological management, action that might previously have been seen as breaching normative requirements is simply prevented by technical means, and questions about the *ethics* of communication are displaced. Normative questions may, of course, arise about decisions to rely on technical measures.

Nor will I discuss the use of digital technologies for specific activities, such as online gambling and gaming, online shopping and marketing, online banking and payment systems,[5] or online security services and record keeping. Each of these and countless other applications of digital technologies raises distinctive ethical issues, and many of them also raise questions about the ethics of communication. Digital technologies can be used to control or monitor industrial and administrative processes; to obtain, record, organise, classify, preserve, analyse, link, disseminate, and suppress data; to measure, monitor and predict aspects of the natural and human worlds and to distribute and market a huge variety of information and services. Each use of digital technologies is likely to raise ethical questions. However, it is not feasible to cover all the ethical issues raised by every application of digital technologies. My focus will be squarely on those that arise in using digital technologies for communication that links human originators to human recipients, and requires not only accessibility and intelligibility, but assessability.

In some cases, the results of activities and systems that use digital technologies for purposes other than communication are then communicated to various audiences, or are made public; in others they are not, or are communicated only if results exceed or fall short on some predetermined critical indicator. Given the gigantic volume of data processed by digital technologies for countless different purposes, this is neither surprising nor avoidable. The ethical issues raised by using digital technologies to communicate with human recipients are numerous, complex and important, and my discussion will be far from exhaustive.

The Wider Context

Regardless of the technologies used, all communication raises ethical questions. All methods of communicating can be (mis)used to deceive or manipulate, to intimidate or defame, and for many other questionable purposes. What matters for the ethics of communication, whichever technologies are used, is whether originators and recipients respect relevant epistemic and ethical norms and standards and can tell whether those with whom they (seek to) communicate do so. Face-to-face speech and technologically mediated speech both lend themselves to ethically and epistemically acceptable and to ethically and epistemically unacceptable types of action. Both can be, and both often are, used not only to inform and communicate honestly and accurately, but to deceive and exaggerate, to distribute propaganda and to defame, to inflate and damage reputations and to exercise covert influence over others' beliefs and action – and for countless other purposes. Ethically and epistemically questionable communication long predates the introduction and spread of digital technologies.

However, new technologies make a difference. They can reshape and extend communication, both for good and for ill. Digital technologies can, for example, be used to influence others in ways that earlier technologies did not support. This is sometimes done by acceptable, even admirable, methods, such as making more (and more robust) evidence and information more widely available. But it can also be done by ethically dubious methods, that rely variously on covert surveillance, blackmail, data theft and identity theft, or that circulate false or dubious claims about selected originators and topics, or target selected recipients with misleading or menacing content. The old familiar speech wrongs, including lying, misleading, distorting and spreading propaganda, not merely remain available and tempting, but have in some ways been reinvigorated and diversified by the availability of digital technologies. In some cases, speech wrongs are reinvigorated by 'targeting' recipients with content that is chosen to persuade, to mislead or to manipulate, while ensuring that originators remain unidentifiable or unknown.

The fact that digital technologies are used for so many purposes other than communication casts some light on the rather awkward vocabularies used to discuss them. These technologies are often referred to as *communication technologies*, ignoring the many non-communicative uses to which they are also constantly put. Sometimes they are rather more accurately referred to as *information and communication technologies (ICT)*, so acknowledging that not all ways of using or processing information are used to communicate. Yet this terminology too may not be apt. As James Williams has pointed out:

> we persist in describing these systems as 'information' or 'communication' technologies, despite the fact that they are designed neither to inform us nor to help us communicate.[6]

This is true, but Williams then suggests that other uses of these technologies aim to produce an 'infrastructure of industrialised persuasion ... and to open a door directly onto our attentional faculties'.[7] This also seems to me correct, but still too narrow. Digital technologies can be used to communicate, and for many further purposes that are neither ways of communicating, nor ways of informing, nor even ways of persuading (which usually involves communication, if sometimes ethically questionable or defective communication).

The broadest, although not the most popular, vocabulary for referring to digital technologies was proposed long ago by Norbert Wiener. He wrote in the preface to the second edition of his classical work *Cybernetics* that when he and his colleagues became aware of

> the essential unity of the set of problems centring about communication, control, and statistical mechanics, whether in the machine, or in living tissue . . . we were hampered . . . by the absence of any common terminology and . . . decided to call the entire field of control and communication theory whether in the machine or in the animal by the name *Cybernetics* . . .[8]

The element *cyber* is now often used in compound terms, such as *cyber intelligence* or *cyber warfare*, *cybercrime* or *cyber bullying*. Here the emphasis is typically on using digital technologies to control or influence, sometimes without communicating with those affected, and sometimes by communication that ignores or indeed flouts various ethical and epistemic standards.

Uses of digital technologies that do not mainly aim to communicate are of huge variety and importance, and raise many questions. However, here I intend to concentrate on uses whose primary aim is to communicate with human recipients, and on the ethical and epistemic standards that matter for that communication. I shall comment both on uses of digital technologies to communicate with individuals, and on their use for public communication that bears on cultural and social life, on scientific and other inquiry, and on public and political life. These communicative uses of digital technologies raise a wide, diverse and significant nexus of ethical and epistemic questions.

2 Acts and Content, Norms and Harms

Speech Acts and Speech Content

Some discussions of the ethics of communication focus on claims about *speech acts*, others on claims about *speech content*. However, a focus on content alone is not enough for an account of the ethics of communication, or of the ethics of digital communication. Unless originators *act* to convey content to recipients, whether individuals or wider audiences, there will be no communication, *a fortiori* no communication of content.

Nevertheless, there have been many attempts to anchor the ethics of communication in claims about forbidden and required speech content. Specific words, symbols or gestures may indeed be required for the valid performance of certain ceremonies or public processes. Examples include oaths of office, marriage ceremonies and religious rituals, where specified content is required by particular cultures, laws or conventions. But the ethics of communication cannot be based entirely on claims that prohibit or require certain speech content in various contexts – even if there is wide agreement about classifying specific content as taboo or blasphemous, or unacceptable in other ways.

Attempts to prohibit types of speech content raise at least two sorts of difficulty. The first is that they are likely to conflict with rights to freedom of expression, and to require oppressive or ethically questionable measures to restrain and penalise those who utter, publish or distribute prohibited content. Control of content has often been enforced by censorship, surveillance or other measures likely to breach not only rights to freedom of expression but other ethical standards, including other human rights.[1] Control of online communication can be harder to detect, and may use or augment evidence obtained by surveillance with powerful data analysis, facial recognition technologies or data location analysis.[2]

A second reason for thinking that a focus on speech content may not offer the best approach to the ethics of communication is that prohibited content can often be replaced with euphemisms or other coded communication that bypasses the prohibitions. Euphemism offers a way of avoiding (supposedly) unacceptable or forbidden speech content, while performing equivalent speech acts. Using euphemisms to voice forbidden claims is nothing new. Montesquieu used it to fine effect in *Lettres Persanes*, when he cast his forbidden critique of the *ancien régime* as an extended commentary on the imagined court of ancient Persia. Although he published no content that was explicitly forbidden, his readers grasped and enjoyed his subversive meaning.

Both organisations and individuals can use euphemistic or coded speech to foil or bypass attempted censorship, and other attempts to regulate content. Euphemism can be used at large and at small scale. It has been used both to evade parts of the mighty censorship apparatus of contemporary China, and to protect the ingenious editorial practices of small satirical magazines – such as *Private Eye* – which would face prosecution if they published explicit versions of actionable claims. The booksellers of pre-revolutionary France used similar tactics to evade censorship of erotic books by marketing their forbidden wares under the unlikely, but well understood, euphemism *livres philosophiques*.[3] Coded communication and euphemism can provide safe ways of communicating and circulating prohibited content. This may not be as glamorous as outwitting the censors by ingenious covert operations, but is both less risky and can be more effective. It works because it complies with explicit prohibitions of certain speech content, yet performs speech acts that can be understood as equivalent to those that contain prohibited content. Controls of speech content still have plenty of advocates – and plenty of practitioners – but do not offer a robust approach to the ethics of communication.

Norms or Harms?

However, it is not enough to focus on speech acts rather than speech content. It is also important to work out *how* a focus on speech acts can best be organised for digital communication. Many current discussions of the ethics of digital communication focus on 'online harms' ('online benefits' are often taken for granted). The term is short for 'harms produced by online activity'. It is evident that some digital communication harms, and some benefits, and that much has mixed effects. However, a focus on harms and benefits may not offer the most useful way of identifying what should be prohibited or permitted.

Circumstances alter cases. Some lies do great harm, but others (including, but not limited to, those that count as 'white' lies) cause little or no harm. Some malicious speech devastates those whom it targets or defames, but some is risible or damages only its originators. Some disinformation campaigns poison public life, but others fail or backfire, or harm their originators. By the same token, speech acts that are accurate or well-intentioned, trustworthy or courteous, often benefit rather than harm, yet sometimes inflict harm. Honouring promises made in good faith often benefits: but honouring a solemn promise of marriage made in ignorance of the fact that the other party is a sibling, or is already married, is likely to harm. Telling the truth often benefits both originators and recipients, yet some truth-telling devastates lives and relationships. Appeals to online harms do not provide an unambiguous guide to action.

Since the harmful and beneficial effects of *proposed* speech acts, including those of speech acts that use digital technologies, often cannot be foreseen, the ethics of communication cannot focus solely on efforts to avoid harm and create benefits. Current discussions of 'online harms', and in particular of harms that might arise from uses of social media, are rightly complex, and for more than one reason.

A lot of current discussion of online harms centres not on proposals to prohibit types of action that are known and shown to harm, or to require types of action that are known and shown to benefit, but rather on *indirect* measures requiring the exercise of care – of caution – by intermediaries who provide and support the relevant activities, including the providers of social media. Legislation of this sort that could mitigate online harms is under discussion in the UK, and elsewhere.[4] The approach likely to be taken recognises the difficulty of predicting the effects of prospective speech acts, and proposes that requirements to exercise *care* be placed on the providers of certain digital and other services – including social media – rather than on individual uses or users of those technologies. If communication that uses those services turns out to harm, then fines can be levied. It remains to be seen how effective this approach can be and it may have different implications for private and public harms.

Private Harms

Some discussion of harms that can be caused by communication, including digital communication, focuses on *private harms* to individuals, and some on *public harms* to shared or public activities. A lot of current discussion of the ethics of digital communication focuses on uses and misuses of various types of social media to post content that may harm individuals, or lead to wider harm. Examples include posts that bully or shame, that breach privacy or make false accusations, and other malicious communication that targets individuals. But harms can also result from digital communication that was not intended to harm individuals.

Careless talk costs lives, but it is often unclear in advance whose lives it may cost. Communication that is intended to harm may fail to do so, and communication that is not intended to harm may do so. The mere fact that some types of communication *may* harm others does not establish enough to focus prohibitions or requirements. Where the incidence of harm cannot be known in advance, a focus on harms may not provide an ethically robust approach to the ethics of communication, or to the ethics of digital communication. A focus on *types* of action undertaken, and on norms or standards that are respected or flouted, is feasible: but a focus on prospective harms is problematic because it is not always possible to predict whether speech acts of a specific type will atually harm.

An adequate account of the ethics of digital communication that centres on requirements to avoid harm would need to take account not only of intended harms, but of unintended and unforeseen harms to individuals. Private harms brought about by others' communication may not be intended, and unintended harms may not be foreseeable. These are compelling reasons for anchoring the ethics of communication, including the ethics of digital communication, not in claims about the results of communication, but in consideration of the types of communicative action undertaken or attempted.

This can be done by focusing on the norms and standards that communication meets or disregards, rather than by trying to predict the beneficial or harmful effects of prospective speech acts. There is – in short, and very inconveniently! – no direct read across from unacceptable action to demonstrable harms. At best we can point to conventional assumptions, which are not borne out in all cases. A dishonest speech act is conventionally *assumed* to harm, and an honest one to do no harm. A malicious comment is conventionally *assumed* to harm, a kindly comment to do no harm. However, these generalisations are shaky. One and the same speech act may be both deceptive and well-intentioned, both mendacious and yet (inadvertently) accurate, and so on. Identifying speech acts as being of a certain type is not enough to show that they will actually lead to harm or benefit in a particular case. But it is often enough to show that action of a certain type respects or breaches some ethical or epistemic norm or standard. A focus on norms and standards for action is not merely better established, but offers a more robust approach to considering the ethical status of communicative action.

Examples of the complex connections between acts and results are readily identified. Many lies harm, but some are 'white' lies that do no harm. Malicious speech intends harm, but some malicious speech does not register, and does not actually harm its intended targets. Disinformation campaigns can damage free elections, but some disinformation campaigns backfire and harm their originators. Equally, when we think that certain speech acts, including digitally mediated speech acts, are accurate or well-intentioned, trustworthy or courteous, we are likely to assume that (other things equal) they do no harm. But other things are not always equal, and there are many examples of communication that does not produce the effects that once seemed likely. Honest speaking can, after all, lead to harm, as can communicating accurate information to those with hostile intentions.

Public Harms

A focus on results, rather than on norms of action, is even more problematic where communication, including digital communication, may lead to *public harms* to culture or science, to the media or democracy. Cultural activities and scientific research, the media and politics, all require inter- action and communication, in which participants are free to express themselves and to listen to others, and to check and to challenge others' claims and assertions. Free speech per- mits and protects communication that proposes and explores claims that *might* turn out to be false, or that *might* damage individuals, institutions and the social fabric. It is often unclear in advance which types of speech act will actually cause, or contribute to, public harms. Speech acts that are neither true nor trustworthy, neither evidenced nor corroborated, sometimes contribute to public goods, or do no harm. That is why the 'wide open robust debate' that public and scientific discussion both encourage permits par- ticipants to put forward and explore false or misleading claims, and to challenge claims that may turn out to be well evidenced. Public debate of all sorts is robust only if it allows for check and challenge to received views. Scientific research must permit – indeed encourage – the articulation, consider- ation and testing of claims that might – or might not – be false. Democratic politics must permit the expression and consideration of positions and proposals that are unpopular or that challenge received views, and that may turn out to be false or misleading.

However, digital technologies can be used, and are sometimes used, to create pseudo-public debate that is insu- lated from genuine check and challenge and is swamped with false, hostile or skewed content. The result may be 'debate' in which participants encounter only the views they already hold, or false information about those who hold other views. A notorious recent example was the use of the platform Parler by some of President Trump's supporters to circulate and promote a false narrative which claimed that the US presidential election of 2020 had been 'stolen'. The platform was penalised only after its users had rioted, entering, occupying and disrupting both the Senate and the House of Representatives.[5]

Public harms are therefore genuinely different. We have reason to tolerate and listen to communication that rejects or disparages established views, that is inaccurate or misleads, in order to ensure that claims about complex public issues are adequately challenged and sifted, substantiating the credibility of those that survive challenge. Equally, scientific research works in part by checking and challenging not only claims whose credentials are widely queried – e.g. the claims of anti-vaccination advocates or flat-earthers – but those of reputable scientists, which earn their credentials by the very fact that they are open to falsification, and will be retracted if falsified.

It follows that warnings that claim that specific types of digital communication would cause 'online harms', or harm democracy, are too simplistic. It can be hard, and may be impossible, to show that specific sorts of communication invariably harm the public interest or public goods, or that they are invariably harmless. It seems unlikely that any simple way of identifying which speech acts harm public goods, or cross some predetermined threshold of harm, can be found. That is why it is sensible to take an indirect approach to online harms by penalising activities that turn out to harm rather than presupposing that harmful communication can be identified in advance.

Norms and Standards for Communicating

None of this is new. Yet – perhaps because a lot of attention has recently focused on harms and benefits rather than on norms and standards – many of the ethical and epistemic standards that matter for communication are either taken for granted, or ignored. Communication, including digital communication, has numerous purposes, addresses varied audiences, and deals with countless topics. So, it is hardly surprising that practical inquiry into the ethics of communication has long since identified and discussed, criticised and promoted, a large number of norms and standards which provide a useful and usable basis for the ethics of communication, including digital communication.

Many of the most discussed norms for communication are *ethical norms* that bear on speech acts. They include norms for duties of various sorts. Some are norms for so-called *perfect duties*, to be respected in all situations. Some, but not all, perfect duties have counterpart rights, and can be claimed by others. These include the two rights bearing on communication that were included in the canonical human rights documents of the mid twentieth century, the right to *freedom of expression* and the right to *privacy*.[6] But other perfect duties that bear on and matter for communication do not have counterpart rights. For example, duties to inform others may not always be matched by rights to be informed; duties of civility may not be matched by rights to civility. In some cases, silence is permissible, and in some that require 'wide open robust debate' making claims that turn out to be false can be valuable.

Many other duties that bear on communication were traditionally classified as *imperfect* (=*incomplete*) duties. Imperfect duties not merely lack counterpart rights, but do not require action in all cases. For example, a duty of *attentiveness* may legitimately be selective: there is nothing wrong with wandering attention where a speaker is endlessly repetitive, and it is not feasible to pay attention to everyone. Or again, a duty of *discretion* requires judgement, and may be set aside in specific circumstances.

Other norms that matter for speech acts, and thereby for communication, are more readily thought of as *epistemic* rather than as *ethical* norms. Examples include *respect for evidence*, for *consistency*, for *accuracy* and for *truth*, as well as norms of *coherence* and *comprehensibility*. However, the division between ethical and epistemic norms for communication is not exclusive. Some of the most important norms for communication, including norms of *consistency*, *truthfulness* and *accuracy*, are widely seen as both ethical and epistemic.

Other norms and standards that bear on communication may be neither ethical nor epistemic. Some might perhaps be seen as *aesthetic norms*, such as *balance*, *simplicity* or *harmony*. Others are *technical* norms and standards that matter for effective communication of specific sorts. Technical norms include not only the generic standards discussed in Chapter 1 (accessibility, intelligibility and assessability), but numerous narrower technical norms, such as *clarity*, *audibility*, *grammaticality*, *legibility*. Evidently, different technical norms will be relevant to communication that uses different technologies or different languages, and some will bear only on digital communication.

And there are also norms that may be thought of as *system norms* that bear on the institutional arrangements for shaping or regulating certain types of communication. These include *transparency* and *freedom of information*. Both have been widely discussed in recent decades, perhaps reflecting the fact that systematic access to information matters more in cultures that are either highly bureaucratised or make extensive use of digital technologies, or both.

Discussions of norms for speech acts, like discussions of other groups of norms, can also be illustrated with examples not of required but of prohibited action. Speech acts may be unacceptable for reasons of all of the above types. They may be inadequate for numerous ethical reasons – for example, because they are instances of *lying*, *perjury*, *deception*, *defamation*, *fraud*, *cheating*, *plagiarism* or *breach of privacy*. They may also be unacceptable because they embody epistemic failings such as *falsity*, *inaccuracy*, *evasion* or *exaggeration*. They may be unacceptable because of technical failings, such as *incoherence* or *incompleteness*. And they may be seen as unacceptable because of *system failings* such as reliance on *surveillance*[7] or on *disinformation campaigning*.[8]

Norms and standards that matter for communication can, of course, also be illustrated by referring either to requirements or to breaches of requirements of all of these sorts. Speech acts may be deemed acceptable if they are accurate or honest, fair minded or well-intentioned, or unacceptable because they are deceptive or defamatory, menacing or mendacious, manipulative or misleading. In judging the ethical and epistemic acceptability of communication we draw on a long list of well-known norms and standards.

Questions of justification can, of course, be raised about each of these norms and standards, and I have spent many years thinking about the considerations that can and cannot play a part in justification. But in this book, I shall not try to justify the ethical and epistemic principles that are central to the ethics of communication, including digital communication. Justification matters, but (as any philosopher knows) it is a time-consuming task that would require a much longer and very different work. Some of the norms and standards that have long been central to the ethics of communication may indeed be questionable, and if so should be questioned. But I see little case for restricting an account of the ethics of digital communication *ex ante* by discarding well-known and well-understood norms and standards without prior consideration.

3   Communication and New Technologies

Norms and Practical Judgement

Whichever communication technologies are used, successful communication must be accessible to recipients, intelligible to them and (in relevant ways) assessable by them. However, communication that meets these technical requirements may fail to meet important ethical and epistemic requirements. Such failures can become harder to detect when established ways of communicating are disrupted by technological innovations: and the digital revolution is not the first example of such disruption. In this chapter I shall look at some difficulties produced by past innovations in communication technologies. These disruptions, and the steps taken to deal with them, may offer clues for addressing the disruptions produced by digital communication technologies.

Changes in communication technology can make it harder for recipients to identify originators, or for originators to identify recipients. If recipients cannot identify originators, and (to a lesser degree) if originators cannot identify the recipients of their communication, it can become harder for them to tell which ethical and epistemic norms and standards are being met, and which are being ignored or flouted.

Once again, the complexity of relevant norms and standards matters. Norms and standards that are of central importance for some types of communication will differ from those that matter most for other types. Scientific communication, for example, fails unless it meets demanding epistemic standards: it must aim for clarity and accuracy, and must seek, take account of and test relevant evidence. Bedtime stories are different: they must appeal to those to whom they are told without including the stuff of nightmares, but need not take account of all the evidence – indeed, they may include and encourage plenty of fantasy. Sports reporting differs from both: it must be accurate (no good reporting losses as wins, let alone wins as losses!), but being partisan is often seen as acceptable.

Although there are many norms that matter for specific sorts of communication, there are also some that matter for a great deal of communication. Regardless of the technologies used, speech acts that make truth claims are seen as ethically inadequate not only if they are used to *lie* or *deceive*, but also if they *defame others*, or are *partisan* or *corrupt*. Speech acts that make scientific truth claims will be epistemically inadequate if they *invent data*, *ignore relevant evidence*, *rely on inaccurate measurements* or are based on *hearsay*. A great deal of communication will be seen as inadequate if it fails to respect norms of *consistency*, *accuracy* and *honesty*.

Communication of all sorts is likely to be seen as ethically defective if it violates prohibitions on *lying, perjury, deception, defamation, fraud, cheating, bullying, manipulation, intimidation, plagiarism* or if it breaches *privacy* or *confidentiality*. Conversely, communication is likely to be seen as meeting ethical requirements insofar as it is *honest, truthful, civil, courteous, trustworthy* and *honours promises*. Communication is likely to be seen as both ethically *and* epistemically inadequate if it *misleads, misinforms, spreads propaganda* or *disinformation*, if it *withholds, ignores* or *falsifies evidence*, or if it spreads *false, inaccurate, evasive* or *exaggerated* claims. And it is likely to be seen as epistemically acceptable insofar it *respects evidence, aims for accuracy*, and *avoids evasion and exaggeration*. There are also norms for communication that bear primarily on recipients rather than on originators, including *attentiveness, discretion* and (once again) *respect for evidence*. Failure to respect these (and other) standards can disrupt and undermine communication and interaction, and that damage can spread far and penetrate deep.

These lists do not – indeed cannot – provide an exhaustive list of ethically or epistemically required or defective ways of communicating: they are neither complete nor completable. They can be extended by listing types of communication that differentiate more, and more specific, prohibitions and requirements. Lying, for example, comes in many varieties. Rory Stewart offers an exuberant list of different ways of lying in a review of Tom Bower's book on Boris Johnson. He writes that Johnson

> has mastered the use of error, omission, exaggeration, diminution, equivocation and flat denial. He has perfected casuistry, circumlocution, false equivalence and false analogy. He is equally adept at the ironic jest, the fib and the grand lie; the weasel word and the half-truth; the

hyperbolic lie, the obvious lie, and the bullshit lie – which may inadvertently be true. And because he has been so famous for this skill for so long, he can use his reputation to ascend to new levels of playful paradox.[1]

This paragraph illustrates perfectly why no list of the norms and standards that bear on communication can hope to be complete.

The ethics of communication is therefore not only complex and demanding, but open-ended. Some complexity arises because different types of communication require respect for different ranges of practical principles. But much of it arises because numerous principles are likely to be relevant to any given case. This means that it is often demanding, and sometimes impossible, to satisfy all the standards that are relevant to each case in all respects.

Norms and standards can conflict, and practical judgement is needed to determine which should be *qualified* in order to meet the claims of others that have weight in the same context. Few, if any, practical principles are unconditional requirements or unconditional prohibitions, and there is no single (let alone algorithmic) method for determining how much weight should be given to each if they cannot be jointly satisfied in a particular context. In some cases, correct information should not be imparted to others in order to avoid a breach of trust; in others it must be disclosed in order to avoid fraud. In some cases, exaggeration will be fun and innocent, in others it may amount to slander.

The indeterminacy of judgement, and specifically of practical judgement, is a feature of all practical reasoning. However, ethical questions about communication are particularly exposed to indeterminacy. Not only are there many types of communication, and many relevant ethical and epistemic norms and standards, but we are often faced with cases in which requirements conflict. There is no avoiding the reality that where it is not possible to satisfy them all, some must be qualified in order to respect others.

Even human rights standards,[2] which are widely seen as normative claims that trump many others, must often be qualified. Deciding which right must be qualified by other rights – and sometimes by other considerations – in particular circumstances is a central task of courts, including international courts. In juridical contexts it is common to speak of *balancing* considerations or of seeking a *proportionate* resolution or decision. But despite the widespread use of these quantitative metaphors in discussions of judicial reasoning, there are no metrics for interpretation, nor therefore for judging which requirements or prohibitions should be modified and which should be upheld in a given case. In cases that come to court, legal experience and judicial reasoning work within a framework of legal requirements and precedents, and carry the burden of judgement. However, most practical judgements are made without resort to legal process, since practical judgement is ubiquitous and indispensable in daily life. Complex situations and potential conflicts between multiple ethical and epistemic (and other) requirements and prohibitions therefore arise not only for judges, but for everyone.

Ancient Norms for Communication

Some of the better-known norms and standards that bear on communication have been discussed and disputed for centuries, and a few for millennia. Among the most ancient examples of norms for communicating are three of the ten commandments. The second commandment prohibits idolatry: *Thou shalt not make unto thee any graven image.* The third commandment prohibits blasphemy: *Thou shalt not take the name of the Lord thy God in vain.* And the ninth commandment prohibits lying or (on some interpretations) specifically lying during a formal process, i.e. perjury: *Thou shalt not bear false witness against thy neighbour.*[3] Although very ancient, these requirements have had continuing importance. The making of graven images has been the focus of dispute and controversy in innumerable later discussions of idolatry, and prohibitions of speech acts that blaspheme, perjure or bear false witness remain important norms for communication.

More recent approaches of the ethics of communication emphasize many further norms, which adds to the complexity of practical judgement. Many twentieth-century discussions place particular emphasis on human rights standards, and in particular on rights to *freedom of expression* and *privacy*. Both of these human rights raise complex questions for communication that uses digital technologies.[4]

However, human rights norms are only a small part of the ethics of communication. Most of the norms and standards that bear on communication are requirements without counterpart rights, among them *honesty, civility, courtesy, discretion, moderation, openness, tact, tolerance* and *trustworthiness*. Beyond specific institutional contexts, respecting these norms may have no legal backing, but these standards are nevertheless seen as strict rather than as discretionary. Other norms for communication bear on systems and structures for communicating, rather than on particular speech acts, among them *security* and *transparency*. This list of norms and standards that bear on communication is far from exhaustive, and it is unlikely that any list could be.

Socrates' Warning

Changes in communication technologies have repeatedly disrupted established approaches to the ethics of communication. The invention and spread of writing, of printing, of film and of broadcasting, each disrupted received views about the ethics of communication. The digital revolution unsurprisingly has added both new and renewed challenges, which are the theme of this book. Some past cases in which communication was disrupted by technological innovation can, perhaps, offer insight into the sorts of difficulties that technological changes can create, and into possible remedies.

Plato writes of an ancient technological innovation that made communication simultaneously more versatile and harder to assess. He tells us that Socrates thought that writing – a technology many had not mastered at the time – was a deceptive and unreliable way of communicating, even for those who could read. In *Phaedrus* Plato reports words that Socrates, who relied entirely on the spoken word, spoke:

> When it has once been written down, every discourse roams about everywhere, reaching indiscriminately those

> with understanding no less than those who have no business with it, and it doesn't know to whom it should speak and to whom it should not. And when it is faulted and attacked unfairly, it always needs its father's [i.e. its author's] support; alone, it can neither defend itself nor come to its own support.[5]

Socrates' complaint is that written words are readily separated both from their authors and from the contexts in which they were produced, making it harder for recipients to understand and assess them. Writing can separate *speech content* from *speech act* and thereby makes it possible to communicate without direct contact between originators and recipients. This is what allows written words to 'roam around'.

However, where the provenance of speech acts is unknown, recipients will often find it harder to assess their meaning, their truth or their trustworthiness, and originators may know less about their audiences (if any). Even those who can read a text may be unsure not merely whose words they are reading, but what the originators intended to convey and whom they meant to address. Detached inscriptions or texts may not reveal *who* produced them, *whether* those originators were trying to communicate, *what* they meant to communicate, or to *whom* they meant to communicate. Lack of information about provenance can make it harder to judge *whether* written claims are true or trustworthy, deceptive or reliable, and whether they satisfy or flout other important ethical and epistemic requirements. Writing obviously creates problems for the illiterate, but Socrates' striking claim is that it also creates problems for competent readers.

The evident and immense advantage of writing is that it enables communication with others who are distant in time and place. Writing expands connectivity. But bridging time and distance by means that obscure provenance and recipience can create risks. Both parties may lack access to matters that would have been readily assessable from tone, gesture or context, or could have been elicited by direct questioning, in face-to-face communication. Lack of information about writers can make it harder for readers to attribute, to follow or to assess what they read, and lack of information about their readers may limit the communication writers achieve. The separation of reader from writer, of recipient from originator, can weaken, even undermine, abilities to understand, interpret, explicate, defend or vouch for the meaning, the truth or the trustworthiness of written words. We can imagine someone in the ancient world finding obscure patterns on a stone surface. He or she might wonder who made them, whether they mean anything, whether they have a purpose, and even whether they have sinister or magical powers.

This is why Socrates concluded that writing creates problems not only for the illiterate, but for those who can read the relevant script or symbols, and consequently not only for readers but for writers. Readers may lack evidence about who the scribes or authors were, who controlled them and what the process of transmission was. They may find it harder to reach reliable views about context and culture, about meaning and origins. If readers are to tell whether written words mean anything, what they mean, and whether what is written is true or false, plausible or far-fetched, evidence-based or imagined, hostile or helpful, information about provenance matters. To assess others' claims and commitments they need to take a view not of the detached speech content – the *ipsissima verba* – but of the speech acts that incorporate, shape and organise speech content: but written words may not make this clear. Decontextualized inscriptions and texts may not provide the information that readers need to judge written words, or that writers use to gauge the reception of their words.

Writing turned out to be a technology with advantages that spoken words lack. Written words create lasting records and preserve information; literary and other conventions can be developed to guide interpretation. Writing makes it possible to have laws as well as customs, books as well as bards. But Socrates was right that without context written words can 'roam around', leaving it unclear who the originators are (or were), and that recipients who cannot discern the provenance of words that they read may find it harder to understand or assess those words.

Readers, Listeners and Viewers

The problems that worried Socrates are an example – perhaps the earliest known example – of ethical issues created by the emergence of new technologies for communicating. Another and better-known example of problems created by new technologies arose with the spread of printing in Europe from the fifteenth century onwards (printing having been invented in China some centuries earlier). Printing extends connectivity and makes it possible to produce and distribute multiple copies of texts. Yet if readers cannot tell who wrote, printed or distributed a text, it can be hard for them to assess its credentials, its reliability or its truth. Without evidence about authors or printers, about origins or transmission, about sources or aims, readers may be left uncertain about the trustworthiness or untrustworthiness, the truth or the falsehood, of printed claims.

However, in this case legislation and regulation provided remedies. Printed material was gradually made more assessable by a combination of legal and cultural innovations that established intermediaries who were required to provide evidence about provenance and authorship, so making it feasible to identify the originators of printed texts and (where relevant) to hold them to account. Across more than two centuries[6] many steps were taken to define and distinguish the respective responsibilities of a range of intermediaries including translators, editors and publishers, printers and book sellers, and the information about provenance that this provided enabled readers and others to distinguish and assess their various contributions.

Needless to say, these measures have sometimes been ignored or breached. All too often, the print media, and in particular the news media – including in democratic states – have been captured and used by parties and factions, by commercial interests and partisan polemicists. When this happens some ethical and epistemic standards for communication may be flouted or avoided in ways which are all too familiar.[7] Early optimism about digital communication and the benefits of wider connectivity make considerable sense in the context of the recurrent reality that some traditional media – including sections of the print and broadcast media in democratic states – repeatedly ignored important ethical and epistemic standards, and that some of them sought to further the interests of owners and their political allies at the expense of the public interest.

Nevertheless, legislation, regulation and culture often resolved some of the difficulties of print communication. These measures *defined* responsibilities for *intermediaries* and *required* them to make themselves *identifiable* in standardised and accessible ways by including an imprint in each copy of a published work or document. Once publishers were required to provide an imprint that conveyed a range of prescribed information, readers could tell not only *who* had written what they read, but also *who* had edited, translated, printed, published and distributed the text, and *where* it had been printed. This provided a basis for readers (and others) to seek redress for failings ranging from defamation to fraud, from forgery to incitement, from breach of copyright to plagiarism. If the relevant originators and intermediaries can be identified, they can (in principle) be held to account for meeting legal, regulatory and professional standards, and these regulatory requirements can be supported by cultural conventions for publishing, selling and marketing various types of text. Taken together, these innovations made it feasible for readers to distinguish reporting from propaganda, fact from fiction, information from disinformation, authors from plagiarists, honest dealers from fraudsters, and so on. These innovations supported assessment of the trustworthiness and untrustworthiness of written texts, without requiring direct contact between originators and recipients.

Regulation that establishes a range of intermediaries and defines their responsibilities also makes it easier to interpret and assess specialised types of speech act. For example, in the UK, and in many other jurisdictions, print advertising too is required to have an imprint that enables those who encounter it to tell *that* it is an advertisement, rather than (more) objective reporting, and generally reveal *who* placed it and paid for it. This can make it possible to seek redress for false advertising. Once provenance is known and originators can be identified, it becomes more feasible to judge the types of speech act involved, to tell whether a specific advertisement is fraudulent or misrepresents the products advertised, and to seek redress for scams and frauds. Similar methods can be used to regulate political campaigning, for example by requiring party political publications to be labelled as such, by regulating financial expenditure for electoral purposes, and by defining and penalising electoral fraud – at least of the more traditional sorts.

Unfortunately, in the UK and in many other jurisdictions, the regulation of political advertising has often been narrowly focused on expenditure by political parties during election and referenda campaigns. These traditional but limited forms of regulation do not enable voters to identify the provenance of political messaging that is produced neither by political parties nor by public-spirited citizens, but by unidentified individuals or organisations with undeclared objectives. They therefore do not address the problem of electoral campaigning by anonymous actors, of whom some may not be citizens, and others may be hostile states: both have become more feasible and more frequent with the use of digital technologies.[8] It is generally accepted that current regulation of electoral campaigning in the UK, and in some other jurisdictions, is insufficient, because it fails to cover anonymous campaigning by non-citizens, including disinformation campaigning and voter deterrence campaigning.[9]

Once radio, film and television became widely used technologies for communication, they too were regulated in democratic societies. Doing so made it more feasible for audiences to identify originators and intermediaries, to grasp and assess their respective contributions, to trace provenance and ultimately to assess and even to challenge misleading content. This provided a basis for assessing the claims made, and for seeking redress or correcting false or misleading, inaccurate or untrustworthy, defamatory or damaging claims.

Traditional Intermediaries

The traditional intermediary structures that were introduced to improve the reliability and assessability of communication that uses older technologies did not restore direct contact between originators and recipients. Nevertheless, they made published material more assessable, and originators more accountable, and enabled recipients to make more confident judgements. Needless to say, these measures were, and remain, imperfect.[10]

The laws, regulations and cultural conventions used to make mediated speech assessable have often been criticised for being too complex, or for failing to deal fully with corruption and conflicts of interest, for focusing on the wrong drivers and issues, or for creating perverse and distracting incentives. Yet in many cases legislative and regulatory measures to create incentives for trustworthy communication, including requirements to identify sources and originators, have worked reasonably well.

However, digital communication currently does not face even the imperfect disciplines that apply to routine uses of earlier communication technologies, including print, broadcasting and film. Printed, broadcast and filmed material can be assessed, and originators can often be identified and (to some extent) be held to account: but equivalent requirements are often lacking when communication uses digital technologies.[11]

One of the main reasons for the absence of parallel disciplines on digital communication is that the technology companies that enable digital communication by providing platforms for various online services are not publishers.[12] Consequently, they are not subject to the requirements and disciplines that publishers face. For example, publishers are required to check the legality of publishing content *before* publication to ensure that it is not defamatory and not in copyright, and also have reasons to protect their reputations by making sure that they do not publish content that ignores or breaches other ethical and epistemic norms and standards.

By contrast, digital platforms, including those supporting various sorts of social media, do not control what is posted on each platform (by members of the public or subscribers depending on the platform), and cannot scrutinise all the material that users post before it is disseminated.[13] Although some platforms seek to identify, to fact-check, to label, and sometimes to take down, material that has been posted, if it is (for example) egregiously offensive or provocative, or demonstrably false, such commitments are both variable and limited.

It is hardly surprising given these realities that there is now a rich literature on ways in which communication that uses digital technologies can damage democracy.[14] That damage takes many forms, including the proliferation of false claims, the organised (re)circulation of disinformation, the promotion of bogus science, and fake news.

Many discussions of digital communication have been slow to engage with these issues. The digital revolution was initially seen as supporting a more deeply democratic future. However, these hopes have unravelled across a decade that culminated in the invasion of the US Capitol in January 2021. In the next chapters I shall consider some of the sources of this striking reversal.[15]

4   Digital Hopes

The Promise of Connectivity

Despite past difficulties with new communication technologies, many greeted digital technologies with high hopes. Enthusiasts thought that the unparalleled connectivity that they provide would support both *wider* and *better* communication between individuals, and lead to better scientific communication and better politics. In particular, many hoped that digital technologies would strengthen and extend democracy by allowing better-informed citizens to participate more fully in public deliberation. Others thought that wider connectivity would make transparency more effective and make a reality of freedom of information.

This did not happen, and there were numerous disappointments and warnings.[1] By 2020 many difficulties had surfaced, and the former CEO of Google, Eric Schmidt, commented acidly that 'The concept of social networks, broadly speaking, as amplifiers for idiots and crazy people is not what we intended.'[2]

There were some good reasons for the initial optimism. Digital technologies can indeed support *wider* communication. They can be used to capture and organise information, to distribute content at unprecedented speed to any number of recipients – or alternatively to target specified audiences, or to suppress content. This can be done at low or no cost to those recipients, and what is distributed may penetrate – even saturate – both public and private spaces. Digital technologies can secure and extend accessibility to a degree that no other communication technology can match.

At first some assumed that the only action needed to realise the promise they saw in digital technologies was to remove obstacles to communication, such as censorship and lesser forms of regulation and restriction of communication that are found even in liberal and democratic jurisdictions. Once those restrictions were removed, enthusiasts hoped, the voice of the people would no longer be marginalised by the voice of the powerful, and this would deepen and strengthen democracy and freedom of expression, and make it easier to hold politicians and other office holders, as well as corporations and their executives, to account. In 2011 these hopes were widely expressed in digitally communicated protest and agitation that challenged existing authorities in the name of democratic change in Egypt, in Spain, in Israel and more widely. This optimism was not, however, supported by any worked out account of the institutional demands of stable democratic government.[3]

Many also hoped that digital technologies would prove transformative beyond public life by supporting more inclusive communication in other areas. The technologies seemed ideal for bypassing social pressures for conformity, for spreading information, for supporting more inclusive cultural activity and enrichment, and for making the fruits of science and research available to wider audiences. And some of these hopes have been realised. Digital technologies can provide search engines that make more information available to more people; they allow people to keep in touch with distant friends and family, and to share enthusiasms across the world; they support open access publishing of scientific research, extend educational opportunity, and provide unparalleled access to information (and to disinformation). And their capacity to support virtual communication proved invaluable during the 2020–1 pandemic.

However, widening accessibility addresses only one of the technical requirements for effective communication, and ignores the ethical and epistemic requirements for acceptable communication. Increasing accessibility does not increase recipients' capacities to understand or to assess others' communication, and does not always support effective communication. Widening accessibility does not make it more likely, let alone certain, that digital communication will respect ethical and epistemic norms. On the contrary, digital technologies can be used to spread fake news, conspiracy theories and bogus science more effectively than earlier technologies permitted.[4]

The connectivity that digital technologies provide differs from that offered by earlier technologies that widened connectivity. Print and broadcasting empower originators by enabling them to communicate with large and dispersed audiences, but provide recipients – readers, listeners and viewers – with limited opportunities to respond or to participate in discussion or debate. Digital technologies can enable wide participation, that can empower recipients: but at some cost. The absence of the traditional intermediaries weakens quality control and accountability, and the anonymity that is extended to originators and manipulators protects those who initiate or spread ethically and epistemically dubious content. Digital technologies can indeed be used to support democratic participation in public life, but they can also be used to insert ethically unacceptable, misleading and damaging content into public debate. Not for nothing is the connectivity they provide sometimes characterised as *virality*, since it allows both information and disinformation, both ethically acceptable and ethically poisonous content, to spread like a virus. Connectivity can spread both benefits and damage.

'Breaking' the Intermediaries

These are not the only reasons why early hopes for the digital future have given way to widespread concern and worry. Another significant source of disappointment is that some early claims about the promise of digital communication were simply unrealistic.

Some enthusiasts stressed the benefits of wider connectivity, but ignored its potential costs and harms. Famously Mark Zuckerberg, the founder of Facebook, put forward a dramatic (and subsequently much criticised) view of what was needed for the benefits of digital technologies to be realised. What was required, he claimed, was 'to move fast and break things', thereby removing damaging obstacles to communication.

Zuckerberg's early assumptions about the structures and practices that harm communication are striking. At that time, he seemingly saw the many intermediary structures and practices that organise and discipline communication that uses older technologies as redundant, or even harmful, and concluded that they should be discarded or 'broken'. These included the complex legislation, institutions and cultural practices that had been developed over some centuries to regulate and moderate publishing, journalism and broadcasting, on which public life, and in particular the public life of democracies, depends. At their best, these measures supported journalistic and editorial standards, and promoted public interest journalism, by enabling readers, listeners and viewers to tell who had produced and (where relevant) who had paid for the production and publication of the content they encountered.

This was generally done by requiring published material to carry an imprint – an identifier – that revealed the provenance of books, newspapers, broadcasting, and of print advertisements. Requiring imprints both incentivises assessable communication, and identifies the originators or intermediaries who enable communication that is illegal, harmful or breaches ethical and epistemic standards.

The humble imprint is a legal requirement on published material, including (in many jurisdictions) on print advertisements. It can enable those who are misled, maligned or harmed by others' assertions or aspersions to tell who is responsible, and may allow them to seek redress. The possibility of detection, of correction and of exposure creates incentives to limit speech wrongs, by making originators identifiable and thereby making public who is responsible for ethically or epistemically unacceptable content. Imprints make communication traceable, and provide evidence of provenance that can be used by those who seek redress or compensation for communication that misinforms, defrauds, defames, incites violence, breaches promises, violates copyright, promotes false advertising, or fails in other ways. They provide essential information for deterring and rectifying communication that wrongs or damages others.

Since digital communication is not currently subject to effective intermediary arrangements, it often escapes these disciplines and constraints. 'Breaking' these everyday requirements on communication can therefore be damaging. It is likely to make communication *less* assessable, and to privilege originators at the expense of recipients. The routine activities of the traditional intermediaries often support reasonably accurate, acceptable and accountable communication, and discarding or 'breaking' them is likely to undermine measures that help make communication intelligible to and assessable by its audiences, and that create incentives to respect ethical and epistemic requirements. At present, however, those who access online content may not be able to tell who produced or paid for it, or how it was distributed.

One result has been considerable uncertainty about the extent to which some democratic elections have been corrupted by online interventions, including interventions by hostile governments. In 2016 concern focused on the role of the (now defunct) company Cambridge Analytica in the campaigns leading up to the Brexit referendum in the UK and the election of Donald Trump as president of the USA. Since 2016 other examples of covert campaigning have come to light.

So, Mark Zuckerberg had a point, but a limited point. The destruction of intermediaries that damage, prevent or distort communication was indeed desirable. Both powerful states and powerful non-state actors, from the Inquisition and traditional dictatorships, to contemporary totalitarian regimes and fraudsters, have often aimed to prevent, constrain or control communication, including political and economic communication. In totalitarian jurisdictions the traditional intermediaries were (and are still) able to suppress communication of which the regime disapproves. They do so by a gamut of measures ranging from intrusive legal and regulatory requirements, to outright censorship, to systematic propaganda and intimidation, sometimes backed by torture and death.[5] However, in less oppressive jurisdictions intermediaries have often helped to secure reasonably reliable editorial and journalistic standards and to ensure that a plurality of voices can be heard, thereby enabling rather than suppressing or distorting public debate and communication, and supporting a range of ethical and epistemic standards. The picture is therefore varied. Intermediaries in some jurisdictions have suppressed or penalised others' communication, and continue to do so. Those in less oppressive jurisdictions have often supported robustly diverse communication, a lot of which meets ethical and epistemic standards, and continue to do so.

Zuckerberg's slogan in effect assumed that the traditional intermediaries had *only* done harm, so that 'breaking things' to secure disintermediation would improve communication. But that was not the full story. This assumption reflected a libertarian outlook that emphasises the importance of freedom of expression, but pays less attention to other ethical and epistemic requirements. Many traditional structures enabled and protected communication, and have benefited democratic, cultural and social life and scientific inquiry. Removing intermediaries does not guarantee better communication, and may damage communication.

Misgivings and Criticisms

Misgivings about Zuckerberg's slogan have been widely discussed for some years. Many criticisms of his early position are summarised in the revealing title of Jonathan Taplin's 2017 book: *Move Fast and Break Things: How Facebook, Google and Amazon Cornered Culture and Undermined Democracy.*[6] Some are discussed at length in the fiercely critical (if more economically titled) *Zucked* by Zuckerberg's one-time mentor and investor, Roger McNamee. These criticisms have now been widely accepted, and Facebook has retired its former inflammatory slogan.

Cultures, Taplin argued, have been 'cornered' by bypassing or undermining structures that required and supported the traditional intermediaries, who had routinely helped to shape and discipline communication. Online communication is neither dominated nor moderated by those intermediaries. The routine contributions of writers and journalists, editors and publishers, newspapers and broadcasters, lawyers and reviewers, have been reduced, bypassed or simply set aside.[7]

The traditional intermediaries had failings, and sometimes prevented, fabricated or distorted communication:

but in many cases their contribution was constructive. In democratic jurisdictions they routinely composed, disciplined, edited, curated, diversified and distributed much of the content that citizens read, heard and viewed, and relied on to test their own and others' claims and assertions. The traditional intermediaries often enabled and supported, rather than suppressed, public reception, interpretation and assessment of content, and thereby supported public interest journalism, public life and democratic institutions. Their contributions shaped and disciplined publishing, serious journalism and broadcasting, and helped maintain standards for communication. This was supported by the routine working of other traditional intermediaries, including reviewers and editors, librarians and researchers, who helped to secure respect for ethical and epistemic standards.

Unsurprisingly, the claim that the vast gain in connectivity that digital technologies offer would automatically strengthen democracy and improve public and professional life, was called into question, including by leading proponents of those very technologies. Sir Tim Berners-Lee, inventor of the World Wide Web, put matters forthrightly in September 2018 when he stated that his early hopes for the Web had been disappointed. He wrote:

> I've always believed the web is for everyone. That's why I and others fight fiercely to protect it. The changes we've managed to bring have created a better and more connected world. But for all the good we've achieved, the web has evolved into an engine of inequity and division; swayed by powerful forces that use it for their own agendas . . . [8]

Intermediaries and Democracy

Today we might wonder why Zuckerberg's slogan was not immediately dismissed as implausible. Why did it ever seem likely that expanding connectivity, let alone being guided by the slogan 'Move fast and break things', would be entirely beneficial, let alone sufficient, or that it would support or deepen democracy? Communication also requires intelligibility and assessability, and acceptable communication requires respect for ethical and epistemic standards. Connectivity is simply not enough for acceptable communication. Democracy, in particular, needs far more than connectivity and the possibility of citizen participation.

The fantasy that connectivity would support not only more, but better communication, and would spread and deepen democracy, perhaps makes sense if one assumes an exaggerated, indeed inaccurate, view of the problems to be addressed. If *all* the intermediate structures and practices that were to be 'broken' had been harmful or useless (as some no doubt were), breaking them would have been a promising start. In short, Zuckerberg had a point, but quite a limited point. In fact, intermediaries *of the right sorts* were needed to protect and discipline communication. Some of the practices and processes that digital technologies broke, bypassed or diminished had enabled and protected cultural and political life; and some were indispensable for democracy.

Expanding connectivity without considering the other technical, ethical and epistemic requirements for communication allows, indeed favours, communication that breaches or ignores a range of important standards. Taplin describes how this took place in some detail. Cultures, he argues, have been 'cornered' by diverting funding and undermining the structures that supported some of the traditional intermediaries whose work had disciplined communication in ways that (generally) improved it and made it more assessable by recipients. The digital revolution made it possible to reduce, bypass or eliminate many of the contributions of writers and journalists, of editors and publishers, of newspapers and broadcasters.[9] These traditional intermediaries had composed, disciplined, edited, curated, diversified and distributed content that members of the public read, heard and viewed. On the whole – although not invariably – they had enabled and supported rather than suppressed the reception, the interpretation and the assessment of printed, broadcast and other material, and thereby supported public debate, scientific research and democratic politics.

The declining numbers and earnings of professional writers and journalists, of publishers and of serious newspapers, provide striking corroboration of these claims.[10] So too does the rise of 'influencers', whose communication overtly prioritises persuasion. The rise of populist politics, often fuelled by digitally enabled (dis)information campaigning, has spread the damage – and the damage has in turn supported populist political movements. Merely 'breaking' the traditional intermediaries may have had some benefits, but clearly also had large costs that damaged standards of communication.

Disintermediation can damage democracy, and disintermediation on its own can do so rapidly and effectively.

Democracy is not just a matter of free and fair elections in which all citizens can vote, thereby ascertaining 'the will of the people' at a given moment.[11] Successful and sustainable democracies temper and check the views and votes of citizens with complex stabilising and filtering institutions. They rely on checks and balances, rather than on unmediated popular control of political decisions. They require *order* (rather than anarchy), rely on the *rule of law*, maintain versions of the *separation of powers*, protect the *independence of the judiciary* and respect (at least) the *elementary rights of the person*. Unmediated direct democracy endangers political stability, and can degenerate into mob rule. The risks of democracy without constitutional restraints have been discussed since Plato wrote about them in *The Republic*, and were well understood by those who have drafted constitutions, including the founding fathers of the United States. They have recently been illustrated all too vividly with the rise of populist movements and politics from the Philippines to the presidency of Donald Trump.

So, any case for 'breaking', or even for curbing, the traditional intermediaries falls far short of a general case for eliminating the disciplines that they can bring to communication, including political communication. It is true that *some* intermediaries did not protect standards of communication, and in *some* cases damaged, skewed, suppressed or censored public discourse, and thereby breached rather than supported ethical, epistemic or other norms and standards that matter for public discourse, and thereby for culture, for science and democracy. But this is not universal, let alone inevitable.

Disintermediation that destroyed *only* damaging or unjust restrictions and constraints on communication would, of course, be worth having. But disintermediation that removes all institutional and cultural checks, balances and constraints on policy making, is more likely to damage than to support democracy. It is hardly surprising that removing the traditional intermediaries does not always benefit democracy or citizens, and can undermine practices and cultures that support democracy. The established, if imperfect, systems of legal, regulatory, professional and cultural quality control, and the intermediaries on which they rely, were devised over some centuries, and often enable, support and discipline public debate, political life and media practices. Although these traditional intermediaries have been far from perfect, the case for marginalising, let alone abolishing, them was not made.[12] Disintermediation does not always or automatically secure either better or more reliable communication, or support democracy, and not all destruction is creative.

Accessibility, in short, is not enough. It is one, but only one, of the technical preconditions of communication. By itself, increasing accessibility by expanding connectivity does not ensure better communication, or secure sustainable democratic politics. The ethics of digital communication also needs to take account both of other technical standards, and of a wide range of ethical and epistemic norms and standards. In the next two chapters I shall comment on some of the central ethical and epistemic standards that matter for communication. I shall first discuss freedom of expression and the right to privacy, which are the two human rights that bear most evidently on communication, and in the last chapter I shall consider some of the risks of protecting and promoting anonymous digital communication.

Part II

Norms and Standards in a Connected World

5   Duties and Rights 1: Freedom of Expression

Rights Before Duties: Historical Sketch

Digital innovations are not the only changes that have reshaped the ethics of communication. A generation or more before the digital revolution, ethical discussion was disrupted by challenges of quite a different sort. Until the twentieth century, discussions of norms and standards in Western cultures were embedded in ethical and cultural traditions that saw duties as fundamental. Ethical discussion addressed the agent's question 'What ought I (or we) do?', and aimed to identify and to justify required and prohibited types of action. Discussions of the ethics of communication followed this pattern. They covered a wide variety of duties and prohibitions that bear on communication, ranging from requirements to speak honestly, to keep promises and to respect evidence, to prohibitions of deceit and defamation, disinformation and discourtesy, and many others.

However, this traditional focus on a broad range of duties was first questioned, then widely rejected, in the aftermath of the First World War. At the start of the war it had still been usual to see duty as fundamental to ethics. Patriotic duty was often seen as exemplary, and Horace's well-known line 'Dulce et decorum est pro patria mori' was quoted with approval.[1] After the war had led to the slaughter of a generation, admiration for patriotic duty was widely rejected, and sometimes derided – notably in Wilfred Owen's famous poem 'Dulce et Decorum est', which dubbed this long tradition 'the old lie'.[2]

This change was later generalised, and between the wars rejection of patriotic duty expanded into wider unease about duties. In the 1930s this unease grew, and made its mark in philosophical writing, when the logical positivists dismissed not only duties but the whole of ethics (and a good deal else) as 'literally meaningless'. If ethics was rejected, did it follow that ethical standards were merely subjective? Claims that ethics is 'merely subjective', a matter of 'my values' or 'my principles', indeed became more prominent, yet did not offer a stable position.[3]

A less subjective response to the eclipse of duty emerged when the horrors of a second World War made strengthening support for ethical standards a matter of urgency. In the 1940s some parts of the traditional ethics of duty were reinforced but others were set aside. This was done by shifting perspective from that of agency to that of recipience, and treating rights rather than duties as fundamental. Duties with corollary rights were reaffirmed, those without counterpart rights were set aside.[4]

If all duties had had correlative rights, a shift of perspective from prioritising agents and their duties to prioritising recipients and their rights would have had few practical implications. However, traditional ethical discussion had covered many duties without counterpart rights, and these were marginalised or ignored once rights were taken as fundamental.

Discussions of duty had traditionally distinguished *perfect* (=complete) from *imperfect* (=incomplete) duties.

Perfect duties – keeping promises, refraining from lying or blackmail, and many more – were seen as 'complete' because they are not discretionary. They require action in any relevant situation and do not permit exceptions in favour of inclination. Imperfect duties, by contrast, leave agents some discretion over whether or not to act in relevant situations. Since duties with counterpart rights are claimable, they are not discretionary, so must be perfect duties.

However, there are also perfect duties that bear on communication but lack counterpart rights, so cannot be claimed by others. These duties are not discretionary (if they were they would be imperfect duties). Examples include duties to self, and many epistemic duties such as duties to listen or pay attention, duties not to exaggerate and many others, as well as other duties that bear on communication such as civility or decency. Few would see these as optional requirements, yet although they are not discretionary, they are not claimable and are not matched by counterpart rights. According priority to rights rather than duties had profound implications for the ethics of communication because it ignores both *imperfect* (=incomplete and discretionary) duties, and perfect duties without counterpart rights.

These distinctions between types of duty are now seldom mentioned in everyday ethical discussion, but remain clear and interesting. The reason that they have fallen into disuse is, it seems, largely that it has become usual to look at ethical norms and standards from the perspective of rights, rather than of duties, hence from the perspective of *recipience* (or more specifically of *claimants*) rather than of *action*. Once the classical agent's question,

'What ought I (or we) do?' was replaced with versions of the recipient's question 'What are my rights?' (more crudely 'What am I entitled to?' or 'What ought I get?'), duties without counterpart rights were easily marginalised and likely to be overlooked. Treating rights rather than duties as fundamental offers a narrower view of ethical requirements, and has striking implications for the ethics of communication.

The Turn to Rights: Freedom of Expression

Digital communication technologies have emerged since the middle of the twentieth century, and a focus on rights has shaped, even dominated, many discussions of the ethics of digital communication. Although it is far from obvious which of the many ethical and epistemic norms and standards that can bear on digital communication matter most, human rights principles are widely seen as central. Yet, they are evidently far from sufficient. A consequence of treating rights rather than duties as basic is that discussion of the ethics of communication, including digital communication, has increasingly focused on a remarkably limited number of ethical and epistemic norms and standards, and in particular on just two human rights.

The *Universal Declaration of Human Rights* (*UDHR*, 1948) and the *European Convention on Human Rights* (*ECHR*, 1950) both include rights to *freedom of expression* and to *privacy*, which evidently bear on communication. I shall comment on these rights in this chapter and the next, but will bracket current disputes between those

64

who hold that rights are fundamentally moral and those who think that they have only political backing.[5]

Article 19 of the *Universal Declaration of Human Rights* gives the right to freedom of expression a famously succinct formulation:

> Everyone has the right to freedom of opinion and expression; this right includes freedom to hold opinions without interference and to seek, receive and impart information and ideas through any media and regardless of frontiers.

The formulation is striking partly because it seems to anticipate technologies that emerged decades later, when digital technologies revolutionised capacities to 'seek, receive and impart information and ideas through any media and regardless of frontiers'.

The most notable feature of the right to freedom of expression is that it is in the first place a right to *hold* and *express* content, including opinions and ideas, and secondarily a right to communicate information. Freedom of expression is of course not merely a right to *self*-expression,[6] but a right to hold and express content that bears on all communication – and yet the text of *UDHR* Article 19 mentions communication of information only as a secondary matter. Many earlier discussions of rights to *free speech*, to *press freedom*, to *religious freedom* and to *academic freedom* had seen these as rights that matter for originators, but did not see originators primarily as 'expressing' content, or treat communication with others as an afterthought. In particular, where the exercise of rights bears on significant public goods, including democratic public life, reliable and informative media, trustworthy cultures and institutions, and competent research and inquiry, rights to communicate with others are of huge importance.

The slightly later formulation of the right to freedom of expression in the *European Convention on Human Rights* does rather more to recognise the importance of recipients as well as of originators, but it too privileges originators. It has two clauses, the first stating what the right protects, the second qualifying those protections. The first runs:

> Art 10.1. Everyone has the right to freedom of expression. This right shall include freedom to hold opinions and to receive and impart information and ideas without interference by public authority and regardless of frontiers. This Article shall not prevent States from requiring the licensing of broadcasting, television or cinema enterprises.

Despite the reference to *receiving* information and ideas, the focus is again very much on the rights of originators. Curiously, the human right that refers most explicitly to communication with others is probably the right to freedom of religion.[7]

However, the second clause of Article 10 as formulated in *ECHR* acknowledges that freedom of expression must be qualified in many ways in order to respect not only other human rights, but a wider range of ethical and epistemic requirements:

> 10.2 The exercise of these freedoms, since it carries with it duties and responsibilities, may be subject to such

66

formalities, conditions, restrictions or penalties as are prescribed by law and are necessary in a democratic society, in the interests of national security, territorial integrity or public safety, for the prevention of disorder or crime, for the protection of health or morals, for the protection of the reputation or rights of others, for preventing the disclosure of information received in confidence, or for maintaining the authority and impartiality of the judiciary.

Communication or Expression?

The change of terminology from a focus on *freedom of speech* to a focus on *freedom of expression* in both human rights documents is, I think, significant. It is a change that treats the expressive use of speech as primary, and its communicative uses as secondary, thereby stressing the rights of originators but paying less attention to the needs or the rights of recipients. Communication, however, requires more than rights that protect expression: it also requires originators to reach recipients who must be able to understand and assess what is communicated. Everyday communication works only if it actually links speakers to hearers, writers to readers, performers to audiences.

Communication between individuals works only if originators and recipients respect a range of interlocking requirements. Originators who respect ethical and epistemic standards must enable recipients to assess and interpret their communication, and to judge which ethical and epistemic requirements are respected, and which are flouted. Communication that aims to address or engage wider audiences, including that required for democratic politics, for the media, for scientific research, and for public and cultural activity, requires respect not merely for freedom of expression, but for many other norms and standards that bear on inquiry and debate.

Why, we may wonder, was the long-standing view that communication, rather than expression, was central to an account of free speech given reduced prominence in the era of human rights? One reason was perhaps that the proliferation of new communication technologies during the past century and a half had made parts of the traditional vocabulary seem awkward. The successive invention and spread of telegraphy, telephony, fax, radio, film and television in the century before digital technologies emerged, and their widespread use, meant that some neutral term was needed. Terminology that referred to specific technologies or institutions – *press freedom*, *freedom to publish*, *freedom of the airwaves* and indeed *political freedom* – could seem narrow or outdated. However, the choice of the phrase 'freedom of expression' as a generic, supposedly technology-neutral, term to cover rights that bear on communication was, I believe, unfortunate. In expressing matters there is no requirement to be or to seek to be accessible to, intelligible to or assessable by others: what is expressed need not be communicated successfully to anyone. Communication, however, requires originators to do more than express content.

Circumstances Alter Cases

It is hardly controversial that originators must be free to express content: if they were not, there could be no communication. But there are good reasons (as well as bad ones) for qualifying this right. Even the most famous and distinguished proponents of rights to freedom of expression have argued for qualified accounts of this right.

For example, John Stuart Mill famously argued for a strong view of rights to express content (which he distinguishes from rights to *self*-expression), yet sees expression of content as a matter of communication, and as needing to meet further requirements:

> the peculiar evil of silencing the expression of an opinion is, that it is robbing the human race; posterity as well as the existing generation; those who dissent from the opinion, still more than those who hold it. If the opinion is right, they are deprived of the opportunity of exchanging error for truth: if wrong, they lose, what is almost as great a benefit, the clearer perception and livelier impression of truth, produced by its collision with error.[8]

Mill concluded that this right must be qualified. His well-known illustration of an acceptable reason for limiting freedom of expression points to the harm speech acts can inflict. He wrote:

> An opinion that corn-dealers are starvers of the poor, or that private property is robbery, ought to be unmolested when simply circulated through the press, but may justly incur punishment when delivered orally to an excited mob assembled before the house of a corn-dealer, or when handed about among the same mob in the form of a placard.[9]

The difference between the cases is that in the latter circumstances these words are 'such as to constitute ... a positive instigation to some mischievous act'.[10]

A similar, and again well-known, illustration of reasons for qualifying freedom of expression in certain circumstances was proposed by the American jurist Oliver Wendell Holmes, who wrote:

> the character of every act depends upon the circumstances in which it is done. The most stringent protection of free speech would not protect a man in falsely shouting 'Fire' in a theatre and causing a panic . . . The question in every case is whether the words used are used in such circumstances and are of such a nature as to create a clear and present danger that they will bring about the substantive evils . . . It is question of proximity and degree.[11]

Many discussions of the ethics of communication refer to these celebrated formulations of acceptable reasons for qualifying rights to free speech, and conclude that expression of content that would cause harm, or imminent harm, or is a clear and present danger, may be prohibited or restricted. But the fact that some communication is likely to harm others, while providing a prima facie reason for prohibiting it, does not show that the *only* reason for prohibiting or regulating communication is that it is likely to harm others. Speech that violates ethical and epistemic requirements sometimes harms, sometimes produces a mixture of harms and benefits, and sometimes secures overall benefit. Ethical claims about freedom of expression must take account of ways in which a variety of other ethical and epistemic norms and standards may qualify rights claims in particular circumstances – as acknowledged in *ECHR* Article 10.2. They do not throw all the weight on predicting whether prospective communication of some type will harm, or whom it will harm, in a particular context.[12] The canonical human rights documents open the way to considering how freedom of expression may and should be qualified, yet may not take full account of the range and complexity of the ethics of communication.

Private and Public Harms

Appeals to prospective harm can be useful in some cases, but are much less so in others. Where speech acts are *intended* to inflict *private harms* – harms to individuals – a focus on harms can be useful for working out which communication should be prohibited, regulated or protected.[13] Comments posted on social media platforms are indeed sometimes intended to harm individuals, for example by promoting suicide or anorexia, by body-shaming or bullying, by distributing violent or pornographic content, or by slander and defamation. However, arguments that appeal to requirements not to harm individuals will not cover all cases.

It is notable that many of the ethical and epistemic norms and standards that bear on communication, and have long been taken seriously, are ignored in the human rights documents. Yet requirements and standards such as honesty and truthfulness, courtesy and civility, or aiming for accuracy and clarity, and many other ethical and epistemic standards that have no counterpart rights are vital for communication that is not merely intelligible and assessable, but ethically and epistemically acceptable.

An assumption that rights to freedom of expression and privacy are *all* that matters is particularly implausible when communication bears on public goods, including democratic governance, public affairs, cultural activities and scientific research. As Bernard Williams reminded us, the epistemic and ethical requirements for communication that aims at truth are substantial:

> in institutions that are expressly dedicated to finding out the truth, such as universities, research institutes, and courts of law, speech is not at all unregulated. People cannot come in from outside, speak when they feel like it, make endless irrelevant, or insulting, interventions, and so on; they cannot invoke a right to do so, and no-one thinks that things would go better in the direction of truth if they could.[14]

An excessive, let alone exclusive, emphasis on freedom of expression is strikingly inadequate not only for ethically and epistemically acceptable communication that makes truth claims but also for communication that bears on public policy, including democratic politics. Freedom of expression is needed in these and many other contexts, but is seldom all that matters.

An excessive focus on rights to freedom of expression, combined with lack of attention to other ethical and epistemic norms, provides part of the context for aggressive contemporary culture wars. On one side, libertarians advocate unrestricted freedom of expression and claim that a great many ways of qualifying rights to freedom of expression simply breach that right. Some of them maintain that permitting and protecting speech acts that misinform or disinform, or that foment discord, are required in order to protect freedom of expression. Their opponents – both 'woke' and merely politically correct – sometimes support excessive restrictions on freedom of expression by demanding legislation that prohibits or penalises 'offensive' speech of various types. Yet since offence is in the eye of the beholder, neither taking offence at others' speech, nor seeing oneself as a victim of their speech acts, can show that action or speech to which offence was taken went beyond what rights to freedom of expression permit. Neither libertarian nor politically correct views of freedom of expression engage with a full enough account of communication, or of the ethics of communication.

Scientific inquiry too requires freedom of expression, but again duly qualified freedom of expression that takes account not only of the complexity of communication but of a wide range of relevant norms and standards. Scientists indeed need to be free to communicate and to publish their findings, but scientific communication also requires respect for many other ethical and epistemic norms and standards. These include respect for evidence, openness about the methods used to seek evidence, respect for claims others have established and honesty about all, including unexpected, experimental results. Research ethics covers these and many other detailed and demanding requirements, and penalties for breaching even the less central ethical and epistemic duties can be substantial.[15]

Democratic debate too requires more than unqualified freedom of expression for citizens. Most evidently, it demands respect for others' political claims and communication: attentive listening as well as robust expression of views. Democratic governance also requires institutional structures that bear on and protect communication in numerous ways.[16] Freedom of expression is indeed indispensable for democracy, as for other activities and purposes, but it provides only a starting point for an account of the ethics of communication in democratic political life.

Yet enthusiasts for freedom of expression, and more generally for a rights-based approach to ethical norms and standards, often ignore other important requirements for democracy. The spread of libertarian versions of populism in some parts of the world in the first two decades of the twenty-first century both rests on and has promoted narrow views of the ethics of communication, in which freedom of expression is seen as central, but other standards for ethically and epistemically acceptable communication are ignored or perhaps taken for granted. In the most problematic cases, combining exaggerated conceptions of freedom of expression with digital connectivity has promoted the proliferation of fake news, spiralling disinformation, filter bubbles and conspiracy theories. All of these may foster cognitive fragmentation and threaten the integrity, and even the future, of a democratic public sphere as well as respect for scientific and other research. Too often the hopes for better and wider communication with which digital technologies were first greeted have been undermined not only by their misuse, but by an ethical focus that sets too much store on a narrow account of ethical standards that is centred on a limited number of human rights.[17]

6 Duties and Rights 2: Rights to Privacy

Privacy Overview

T he right to privacy is the other human right that bears on communication, although not only on communication. Its formulations in the *Universal Declaration* and in the *European Convention* are very similar and quite dated. Although privacy is often discussed in conjunction with other informational requirements, such as transparency, confidentiality or freedom of information, none of these are counted as human rights. And once again, concentrating on one specific right may offer a limited contribution to the complex ethical and epistemic standards that are relevant to communication, and especially to digital communication. Digital technologies raise numerous challenges for privacy, and addressing them is likely to require attention to a wide range of ethical and epistemic norms and standards.[1]

In Article 12 of the *Universal Declaration* the right to privacy is set out in the words:

> No one shall be subjected to arbitrary interference with his privacy, family, home or correspondence, nor to attacks upon his honour and reputation. Everyone has the right to the protection of the law against such interference or attacks.

In Article 8 of the *European Convention* the right to privacy is once again set out in two clauses, the first repeating the *UDHR* formulation by specifying what is to be protected, and the second setting out a selection of qualifications of those protections:

1. Everyone has the right to respect for his private and family life, his home and his correspondence.
2. There shall be no interference by a public authority with the exercise of this right except such as is in accordance with the law and is necessary in a democratic society in the interests of national security, public safety or the economic well-being of the country, for the prevention of disorder or crime, for the protection of health or morals, or for the protection of the rights and freedoms of others.

Both these and other accounts of the right to privacy see it as protecting capacities to act. They centre on quite traditional views of violations of privacy that include interference with a person's 'privacy, family, home or correspondence'. Unsurprisingly, given that they were drafted long before the digital revolution, neither refers to digital technologies or to data. Indeed, the reference to *correspondence* is the only indication that rights to privacy bear on information or communication. However, in the digital age discussions of rights to privacy have concentrated very largely on informational privacy.[2]

There are countless ways of interfering with others' privacy.[3] Interference can be achieved by *intruding* into their private space, by *intercepting or accessing* their private communication or by drawing *inferences* that reveal matters that were intended to remain private. Digital technologies have made informational privacy more vulnerable, and its protection more difficult. Personal information is held both by individuals and by organisations, often without the relevant data subjects knowing which information is held by whom. Much will be held in digital form, and some in traditional paper records and files; some will be in the public domain, and some will not; data that are not in the public domain may be held under varying terms and conditions. Digital technologies challenge rights to privacy by making it cheap and easy to transmit personal information, and for those who hold data to organise and link different data sets. Unsurprisingly they have often made it harder to ensure respect for rights to privacy.

Both information and misinformation about matters that individuals aim to keep private, whether obtained by intrusion, by interception or by inference, can be disseminated and (assuming the generic technical conditions for successful communication are satisfied) communicated widely and effectively using digital technologies. Content of all sorts can be distributed as rumours and provocations, calumny and gossip, allegations and surmises, and can be transmitted either to selected recipients or to the world at large.

Digital connectivity has greatly complicated the task of protecting privacy by making it easier to infer matters that could otherwise have remained private, and to transmit that information either to individuals or to the world at large. Some breaches of privacy work by drawing inferences from data that individuals access or create when online, but intend to remain private, such as the content of confidential correspondence. Others reveal matters of which those whose privacy is breached are often unaware. For example, agreeing to the use of cookies and clicking on links when using digital technologies can enable access to information about matters that service users assumed would not be available.

Inferences to matters that could otherwise have remained private may also occur when individuals are *not* online, but are merely near to technology that registers who they are, where they are or what they are doing. For example, data can be collected when individuals carry (but are not using) a mobile phone, when they pass a security camera, when they drive along a street, when they enter a building, when they have a conversation in a place where the dreaded Alexa is eavesdropping, or when they engage in many other everyday activities. Each of us leaves a data trail as we move through a world replete with digital technology that collects and preserves information. Once personal data are 'harvested', organised and linked to other data – including any related data that are in the public domain – they can be used to support inferences to matters that could otherwise have remained private. That information may sometimes be made available or sold to others, including data brokers, advertisers and campaigning organisations.

The Point of Privacy

Does this matter? As long ago as 2010 Mark Zuckerberg suggested that privacy was no longer a social norm, and many others have suggested that it is obsolete, or that people (particularly young people) no long care about privacy, or that it matters only to those who have something to hide.

However, there is plenty of empirical evidence that people still care about privacy, and also that young people care about privacy, even if their specific privacy concerns differ from those of older people. In any case, there are good reasons to care about privacy – even for those who have nothing to hide.

If the right to privacy is to protect individuals from 'arbitrary interference', it must ensure that private information does not become more widely available than individuals intend. Privacy requires a reasonable assurance that information reaches intended recipients without becoming available to others, let alone becoming public knowledge. The reason privacy matters is not, however, generally because people have 'something to hide'. Rather it matters because human agency is fragile and communication that spreads information to unintended recipients may lead not merely to embarrassment or ridicule, but to unwanted attention or reputational damage, to loss of friends or of business opportunities, to loss of employment or to political risks.[4] Securing privacy matters because it can protect individuals from interference, intimidation and pressures of many sorts, thereby supporting their capacities to act. Privacy matters particularly where others might use private information to harm or intimidate individuals, or to prevent or undermine their action. Breaches of privacy can create opportunities for blackmail, can undermine agreements and negotiations, can destroy trust and reputations, and can provide others with leverage for making demands or obtaining benefits to which they are not entitled. They provide opportunities for action that uses, or rather misuses, private information by facilitating embarrassment and intrusion, extortion and bullying, fraud and blackmail. This has led some to argue that privacy is power.[5] This may be a claim too far, or at least too easily misconstrued. Privacy is necessary for a degree of security, and can be particularly important for individuals who *lack* power. Individual privacy matters not only for private and family life, but also for professional, business and public life, and for participation in public life, including democratic politics.

Data Protection and 'Personal Information'

The European Union has long made particularly strenuous efforts to protect important aspects of privacy, and to address some of the distinctive problems of securing rights to privacy in a digital age. Measures began with the *Data Protection Directive* (1985) and were updated in the *General Regulation on Data Protection* (*GDPR*, 2016), which was incorporated into the domestic law of member states in 2018. Data protection approaches to rights to privacy aim to restrict access to others' *personal* information unless for specified reasons, by regulating the data policies of larger institutions and requiring them to protect all personal data in their keeping. The regulated institutions must safeguard personal data, and may make them available only for specified purposes, or with permission from the relevant data subjects (those to whom the data refer). For example, data may be disclosed if needed for policing or security; if data subjects consent to their communication; or if they have been effectively anonymised.

Digital technologies provide many ways of 'processing' information, including personal information. However, the term 'processing' as used in data protection legislation does not refer to the fact that a great deal of data processing now uses digital technologies. 'Processing' as defined in data protection law and regulation covers acquiring, recording, organizing, altering, retrieving, linking, consulting or using data *using any communication technology*.[6] Written and recorded material therefore falls under the same data protection requirements as digitised content.

The difficulty of this approach does not, however, arise from this broad definition of 'processing', but from the fundamental requirement to classify data about individuals either as *personal* or as *non-personal*. This distinction is essential for regulating 'personal' information, yet is not easily drawn. The standard approach is to deem information 'personal' if it enables the identification of individuals. For example, in the UK the 1998 Act that incorporated the original EU directive into law characterised personal data as

> data which relate to a living individual who can be identified (a) from those data, or (b) from those data and other information which is in the possession of, or is likely to come into the possession of, the data controller.[7]

This clarifies one matter: data protection does not extend to the dead, to whom it affords no protection.[8] However, information that is true of living persons does not automatically count as personal information. A lot that is true of each of us is information that is true of many others. Each of us has human ancestors and was born at some time in the past. So personal information does not cover all information that is true of persons. Indeed, it does not cover information that is true of many, but not all, persons: many of us were born in the UK, and many of us are over 5 feet tall. This sort of information does not count as personal because it is insufficient to identify individual persons. Yet, when linked to other information, even trivial and commonplace information about persons may make identification possible.

The careful explanations provided on the website of the UK regulator of data protection, the Information Commissioner's Office, seek to explain what it takes for information to count as personal.[9] The crucial element in the legal definition of personal information is that it is information that makes an individual *identifiable* on the basis of 'other information' 'held by, or likely to be held by the data controller'. But since that 'other information' will vary from case to case, the *inferences* that can be drawn from it will also vary. A small and commonplace piece of information about an individual may be the crucial clue that makes her identifiable by those with access to certain other information, as every reader of detective fiction knows. And in some cases, the 'other' information that makes individuals identifiable may be in the public domain.

Personal and Sensitive Information

Many of the earlier discussions of data protection approaches to protecting the right to privacy focused on the protection of personal information in medical practice and research. Medical information about individuals is classified not merely as *personal*, but as *personal and sensitive*, and the need for privacy is evidently particularly significant in this area. Full access to an individual's medical information could, for example, provide a basis for insurance companies to exclude 'higher risk' individuals from insurance, including those who would never experience the condition for which they are (statistically) at risk. It would allow employers to refuse employment to those with indications of conditions that were unlikely to affect their capacities.

So, it is hardly surprising that an emphasis on data that render individuals *identifiable* by others has led to controversy in medical and social research, and to difficulties for those who undertake, fund or use that research. On one view, if medical data are *anonymised* (and there has been dispute about the use of this term) persons are *not* identifiable, and so information that refers to them will *not* count as personal. However, on another view, if anonymisation is reversible, then however secure the encryption and however limited access to the key, individuals will be *in principle* identifiable by *some* means by *some* others. This has led some to think that reversible anonymisation is too weak to satisfy data protection requirements.

This is not a marginal or merely technical issue. If irreversible anonymisation that *delinks* data were needed for acceptable (re)use of medical data (other than for medical treatment of that individual) a great deal of medical and social research, as well as work in public health and epidemiology, including any secondary data analysis, would be impossible without obtaining specific consent from each data subject. Unclarity about what makes data *identifiable*, and so *personal*, can hamper medical and social research in fundamental ways. Without linkable data, epidemiology, longitudinal social studies and many secondary data analyses that are relevant to public health, would be difficult, if not impossible.

Yet reversible anonymisation, which does not destroy the possibility of linking information, and is sometimes thought to provide adequate informational privacy, has at other times been seen as incompatible with data protection requirements.[10] Although the UK National Health Service might respond to this claim by ingeniously pointing out that it is the data controller for medical data for the entire population, so that research carried out under its auspices raises no problems, this does not really deal with the underlying problem.

Informed Consent and Personal Data

Reuse of personal data is also permissible if the relevant data subject gives informed consent to a specified reuse. Informed consent requirements have played a large part in medical ethics, and in many other areas of inquiry. They were originally seen as qualifying duties of professional and commercial confidentiality, and later extended to medical and other research, and have been central to important ethical codes for medical practice and research, such as the *Nuremberg Code* (1947) and successive versions of the *Declaration of Helsinki*. Elements of these codes have since been embedded in countless codes of professional ethics for medical practice and research.

However, in the very period during which those who drafted requirements for research ethics tried to make informed consent requirements *more* demanding and detailed, standards for consent were being lowered by relying on digital technologies. Giving informed consent originally meant what it said: those who gave consent had to be *informed*, so had to absorb and understand the relevant information for their consent. That was often possible in clinical practice. But obtaining informed consent in research contexts is often harder, since there is likely to be more and more complicated information. Yet when consent procedures are digital, standards are all too often reduced to what one might fairly call 'tick and click' consent. Those whose consent is sought are asked to provide it by ticking a box in an online form, often without reading, let alone understanding, the content to which they are supposedly consenting.

This approach to consent has been widely discussed and derided. It was mocked by those who concocted a (bogus) consent form with a clause requesting consent to giving one's first-born to the devil: many of those to whom the form was presented did not read the small print and ticked the relevant box. In short, people simply do not read the lengthy requests for consent to which they agree. And there are good reasons not to read them. A 2019 opinion piece in the *New York Times* under the telling (and often repeated) heading 'How Silicon Valley Puts the "Con" in Consent' pointed out that:

The average person would have to spend 76 working days reading all of the digital privacy policies they agree to in the span of a year. Reading Amazon's terms and conditions alone out loud takes approximately nine hours ... The legal fiction of consent is blatant ...[11]

Privacy in Practice

The combination of proliferating consent requirements with insouciant approaches to standards for consent has corroded many approaches to protecting privacy, including data protection approaches.

A different approach to protecting privacy that deserves mention is the idea of providing 'safe havens' for personal information that is needed for population-based research and statistical analysis. The idea combines secure holding of personal data with a system of accrediting researchers who meet relevant criteria to work within those safe havens.[12] Whether bolting exemptions onto current data protection legislation and guidance can provide an ethically robust and effective way of protecting privacy is unclear. Nor is it evident that this 'exceptionalist' approach is required in a world where each patient is treated on the basis of information gained by treating others. Secondly, while the recommendation offers a remedy for some of the problems that an unclear definition of personal data has raised for *medical* research, it does nothing to remedy the problems generated by a defective distinction between personal and non-personal data in other contexts. The problems that arise for access to personal data for population research, and thereby for evidence-based public policy, remain unresolved.

Data protection requirements are relevant to a great range both of research, and of other activities. Elaborate consent procedures could perhaps be devised and implemented for complex research. But procedures are also important in daily medical practice, and beyond medical practice and research. For example, may a doctor *revisit* information obtained by treating past patients before treating a current patient? To do so would ostensibly breach data protection requirements, unless past patients consent – yet securing that consent may not be practicable.

Yet each of us hopes that we will *always* be treated on the basis of information obtained by treating earlier patients. Does anyone have a right to refuse to allow reversibly anonymised information about their own treatment to be used to inform treatment of future patients? Reversible anonymisation is, after all, not enough to guarantee that data subjects remain unidentifiable, so seemingly not enough to meet data protection requirements. My suspicion is that compliance with requirements not to reuse 'personal' information to inform clinical judgement is – fortunately! – poor. There are good reasons for protecting informational privacy, but data protection approaches to doing so have faced and still face difficulties.

Part III

Politics and Connectivity

7   Power and Anonymity

A Turning Point?

Appeals to human rights make an important but limited contribution to the ethics of communication. On reflection this is hardly surprising: communication is complex; the ethics of communication is unavoidably complex, and the ethics of digital communication unavoidably even more complex.[1] Since human rights approaches to ethics appeal to very few abstractly formulated principles, it is important to ask how those principles may and must be qualified to take account of a wider range of important norms and standards.

However, it is far from obvious how to move towards a fuller and more adequate account of the ethical and epistemic norms and standards that matter for communication, or specifically for digital communication, let alone how those requirements can be made effective.

Current discussions of ethical and epistemic standards for digital communication canvas a truly bewildering array of possible interventions and supposed remedies for a wide range of problems to which some uses of digital communication can lead. Some discussions focus on ways of addressing and limiting harms to individuals that can arise from digital communication, often emphasizing those produced by (mis)uses of certain types of social media. Others focus on curbing uses of digital communication that undermine or damage public goods, including cultural and scientific activity, political processes and democratic governance. I shall pay particular attention to the latter.[2]

These debates include many proposals from governments, political parties, international and civil society organisations, corporate and professional bodies, as well as from individual experts, researchers, politicians, journalists and citizens. Although there is some agreement about the problems that digital communication can produce, there is very little about how they could or should be dealt with. There is, however, a note of rising concern, and recurrent disagreement between those who still maintain that regulation of digital communication is an unacceptable restriction of rights to freedom of expression, those who advocate regulation, and those who think that more radical measures, such as anti-trust action to break up the larger tech corporations, will be needed.

These disagreements were vividly illustrated by responses to the riot in the US Capitol on 6 January 2021, which had been coordinated and encouraged by online communication. Some of the larger service providers had previously resisted proposals for regulation (especially of social media) and insisted repeatedly that they were not publishers and should not be regulated as such. Then, faced with this crisis, some of them abruptly took on some of the tasks of editors, and removed access for those who were promoting conspiracies, disinformation and confrontations.

Claims that rights to freedom of expression preclude regulation of digital communication had previously been strongly supported by these very companies. For example, in May 2020 Mark Zuckerberg restated why he believed that Facebook should not edit what users post:

> I just believe strongly that Facebook shouldn't be the arbiter of truth of everything that people say online ... I think in general private companies probably shouldn't be – especially these platform companies – shouldn't be in the position of doing that.[3]

Yet eight months later, Facebook kicked Mr Trump off for stoking riots at the Capitol,[4] while Twitter shut down his account, and the Parler service that his supporters were using to promote and coordinate disinformation, violence and insurrection was disabled (it was later re-established). These companies had long used commercial terms and conditions to exercise some control over the content that they hosted, but insisted that they did not and should not have an editorial role. Almost overnight they took on some of the tasks of publishers. Nor was this new attention to editorial standards limited to the events on Capitol Hill. Almost simultaneously Facebook stated that it would take down deep fakes and denied service to the Burmese military.[5]

These decisions were taken in an emergency, and were controversial even in the eyes of some of those who made them. Jack Dorsey, the CEO of Twitter, tweeted:

> I do not celebrate or feel pride in our having to ban @realDonaldTrump from Twitter, or how we got here. After a clear warning we'd take this action, we made a decision with the best information we had on threats to physical safety both on and off Twitter. Was this correct?[6]

Whether or not it was correct, it was certainly surprising. The decision followed years during which major tech companies had been adamant that they were not publishers and should not be subject to or impose the disciplines that publishers and editors apply to communication that uses older technologies.

A Profusion of Proposals

These dramatic changes made by a few major digital service providers are only a small selection from the innumerable suggestions for regulating online communication that have been proposed and canvassed. Some proposals focus on specific uses or users of digital technologies, others are of wide application.

Among the more anodyne proposals are many suggestions for raising levels of digital literacy: surely a good idea, but unlikely to resolve many of the problems. At the other end of the spectrum are repeated proposals that antitrust measures be used to break up the largest tech companies – and by the end of 2020 there appeared to be some support for such measures.[7] However, most proposals have been neither as anodyne as improving digital literacy, nor as radical as breaking up powerful companies. Many focus on changes that (if feasible) could address some problems that affect digital communication, but would ignore others.

Some advocate more rigorous implementation of data protection approaches to ensure that personal information is not hoarded, (mis)used or transferred without the consent of data subjects. Others argue for greater transparency about the algorithms used to organise and distribute digital content, and for measures to limit algorithmic bias.[8] Some lay store by extending rights to privacy with a 'right to be forgotten' – a right to have certain categories of personal data not protected, but erased.[9] Others suggest that individuals ought to take more effective measures to prevent (mis) appropriation of their personal data. Some suggest that taxing online services in the jurisdictions where they market their services and make profits, rather than where their providers are headquartered, would strengthen levers for change. Others are mainly concerned about the tendency of online communication to generate filter bubbles and echo chambers that shield recipients from views other than those they already hold, thereby damaging public debate and inquiry.[10] Some suggest that fact-checking should be more widely used to identify false claims, which should then be taken down to limit the spread of misinformation, disinformation and conspiracy theories. Others worry that this would infringe rights to freedom of expression, and suggest that labelling false claims provides remedy enough, even if they are not taken down – and some service providers now label content as false, but do not take it down. Others suggest that political uses of online services, like the political use of print and broadcasting, should be required to meet specified standards – but without defining what counts as a 'political use'. Some argue more ambitiously that those who provide online services should take on the full responsibilities of publishers, and stop claiming that they are merely 'common carriers' providing platforms on which others post content, for which they have no responsibility. Some argue that measures to limit online harms inflicted by individual uses of social media are the key to improving respect for standards that matter.[11] Others cling to the first fine careless rapture with which digital technologies were initially greeted, and maintain that neither change nor increased regulation is needed, and that untrammelled online communication is necessary to respect rights to freedom of expression. This list is only illustrative, and it is unlikely that a comprehensive list could be drawn up.

It is evidently not feasible to discuss each of these proposals, to do justice to all the suggested remedial interventions, or to tally the merits and deficiencies of each proposal. Doing so would require a very long book on the feasibility and effectiveness of possible legal and regulatory measures in and across multiple jurisdictions, and would date rapidly. This book is about the ethics, not the regulation, of digital communication, so I shall focus on some of the underlying sources of ethical problems. This I hope will suggest a starting point – but only a starting point – for considering which legal and regulatory measures could be feasible, effective and ethically acceptable.

Accountable Communication and Anonymity

Ways of making digital communication more accountable will inevitably be complex. I have emphasized throughout this book that since communication is complex and varied, the ethics of communication is unavoidably also complex. It must address many sorts of communication, undertaken for various purposes, dealing with varied topics, in differing circumstances, using various languages and registers – and numerous technologies. The norms and standards likely to be relevant include technical, ethical and epistemic requirements that matter for many sorts of communication, as well as narrower requirements that are relevant to specific types of communication. One consequence of this complexity is that it is not likely to be feasible to provide a complete list of principles that matter for communication, let alone for each type of communication. As we have seen, neither a focus on online harms nor a focus on human rights is likely to be adequate.

So rather than trying to list and comment on *all* the norms and standards that matter for communication, including digital communication, I shall identify what I see as an underlying feature of the current organisation of digital communication that bears on the feasibility of taking account of important ethical and epistemic (and other) requirements. This should make it easier to work out which of the countless proposals are relevant and feasible.

As it seems to me, problems cannot be addressed unless those responsible for them can be identified. So long as some of those whose action shapes digital communication can remain anonymous, they *cannot* be held to account. Anonymity matters because it creates a digital version of the problem that worried Socrates. When recipients cannot identify originators, when speech content 'roams around' and does not know 'to whom it should speak and to whom it should not speak', accountability is likely to be difficult or impossible (see Chapter 3). Even where the

content communicated is clearly inflammatory or defamatory, dangerous or deceptive, neither originators nor organisers of communication can be held to account if they
cannot be identified.

There are situations in which anonymity does no
harm. But where those who organise, commission or target
communication that breaches important norms and standards are allowed to remain anonymous, the effects can be
serious. If those with power to control or fund digital communication cannot be identified, it will be hard – perhaps
impossible – to hold them to account even if they promote
false and misleading claims, suppress important information, distort public debate, manipulate evidence or promote
propaganda.

The striking rise of conspiracy theories, from
QAnon to anti-vaccination enthusiasm, from the spread of
fake news to the well-funded activities of climate change
deniers, has increased in the very years in which digital
communication has mushroomed, and offers some sobering
evidence. This matters. As Carisa Vélez puts the point, 'the
moment you think "that's propaganda" . . . the next question
is "who put it there?"'.[12] However, if those who put it there
can remain anonymous, it will be hard or impossible to
answer this fundamental question. The same applies where
ethical and epistemic failings take the form not of propaganda, but of misinformation or disinformation, of incitement or deception. If those who 'put it there', or who pay
and enable others to 'put it there', can do so anonymously,
accountability will not be feasible and legal or regulatory
requirements are unlikely to be effective.

States and Corporations, Customers and Users

The difficulty of tracing who is responsible for ethical and epistemic defects in digital communication arises in considerable part because powerful and influential individuals and organisations can operate anonymously. Digital communication can bring the benefits and pleasures of conversations with distant friends and family, and opens access to a dramatic range of information and entertainment. But it can also support malicious fabrications, systematic denigration, propaganda and conspiracies not only by anonymous individuals, but by groups and movements whose funding and membership are not known, and whose digital communication orchestrates insistent and intrusive exposure to narrow or dubious – yet sometimes appealing – content for those whom it targets. Those who seek to manipulate and misinform, to ramp up hostility and division, should indeed be held to account: but this is feasible only if they can be identified.

Digital technologies provide many ways of shaping and controlling communication without being accountable. In some cases, these technologies are controlled by the security apparatus of powerful states, and in others by non-state actors, including both powerful businesses and some of their major customers. When states control digital technologies and services, power over digital communication is likely to be dangerously concentrated and unaccountable. Surveillance states damage both those within and those beyond their borders, and have done so since long before the digital revolution.[13] State surveillance today uses digital tech-nologies not only to monitor but to shape and control aspects of the cultural, social, economic and (all too often) the entire lives of their inhabitants. State surveillance has a long history, and digital technologies have made it more effective, more intrusive, harder to evade or detect, and thereby harder for victims to hold perpetrators to account.

An overlapping group of problems arises when digital technologies are provided not by states, but by powerful companies. In democratic states businesses that organise digital communication are held to account for some matters, but not for others. They are held to account for complying with standards of corporate governance and specific legal requirements in jurisdictions where they oper-ate or are incorporated. But they are not at present held to account for other aspects of the services they provide. They can provide digital services and make personal data available to customers who use them to target audiences not only with legitimate information and advertising, but with misinfor-mation, disinformation and propaganda. They may enable those customers to damage democracy, corrode cultures, spread hostilities and foster political manipulation: yet it can be difficult or impossible to tell who should be held to account.

In part this reflects an unusual feature of digital services in market economies, which is that the roles of *customer* and *user* can be separated. Service users provide their personal data in return for access – often free access – to specific services; service providers then sell the use of those data to their actual customers, enabling them to reach and target those data subjects with specific content – and in many cases to do so anonymously.

This separation of customers and users is not unique, but until the emergence of digital technologies was on a small scale. A great deal of pre-digital communication, particularly of political and other public content, was made available either to the public at large or to readers, listeners and viewers who were customers of the originators and either paid for the content they accessed or paid taxes that funded it. If those customers found what was provided unacceptable, they could withdraw their custom. Publishers provided books and journals for readers: who were their customers. Newspapers and magazines provided news and other content for their readers: who were their customers. Broadcasters provided programmes for their audiences: who were their customers. Alternatively, public service broadcasters provided programmes for audiences, funded by a charge (a tax or licence fee) paid by or on behalf of listeners and viewers, so once again users had some leverage and some basis for holding originators to account.

There are, of course, acceptable ways of separating the roles of user and customer. Customers can pay for others to receive specified content: gift subscriptions are an obvious, if trivial, case. But this is on a small scale and makes little difference: although the recipient does not pay, someone with his or her interests or preferences in mind pays. For the most part, however, recipients of communication that relies on older technologies have been customers, and originators have therefore had reason to take account of their interests and demands: if they do not, revenues are likely to shrink, even to vanish.

However, users of online services, in particular of social media, are often not customers, and do not pay for the content they receive. Consequently, incentives for originators to take account of the preferences, the interests, or indeed the needs, of recipients are absent. However, the tech companies that provide free services have paying customers. Those customers pay not for access to content, but for access to data provided by users, whom they then seek to influence by targeting them with information or disinformation, ranging from routine commercial advertisements to inflammatory propaganda. Advertisements are likely, for obvious commercial reasons, to reveal who paid for them: communication that spreads propaganda or disinformation or that incites illegal or hostile action is not.

The new business model bypasses many of the types of moderation that traditional intermediaries provided for readers, listeners and viewers. At their best those intermediaries required communication to meet a range of ethical and epistemic standards. Publishers and editors risked prosecution if the communication they organised violated legal requirements (e.g. by defamation, violating copyright, or passing off), and risked reputational or economic damage if they ignored other ethical and epistemic requirements. The new business model is controlled by quite different intermediaries, who sell the power to influence others to powerful but often anonymous clients.

In theory – although not always in practice – the old intermediaries were regulated by law and formed by professional cultures of publishing, including those of public interest journalism.[14] At their best the communication for which they were responsible met ethical, epistemic and other requirements. At their worst, they respected only requirements whose breach risked legal or financial penalties, and ignored other important standards.

However, many of the new intermediaries are invisible both to those whom they target and to the wider public, and face few effective requirements and incentives. They have an interest in ensuring that communication works, and therefore in its being accessible, intelligible and (up to a point!) assessable for the audiences they pay to target. But they may not be concerned to ensure that the content that they host – or ghost – respects the full range of ethical or epistemic standards that matter for communication, for public interest journalism or for democracy. The new intermediaries make their money by selling the means of influencing, and often gain advantage by ignoring and bypassing those standards. They process, repurpose and market data obtained from service users to customers whose aim is to persuade those users.

The business model is simple. Service users 'allow' their personal data to be used[15] in return for receiving 'free' digital services, while service providers make their return by linking, organising and selling data obtained from service users (often combined with data that are in the public domain) to customers. The 'products' may include both targeted advertising of commodities, and targeted political and social messaging, some of which may consist of disinformation, promote conspiracies, or damage democratic process. Unsurprisingly providers of digital services are likely to be more responsive to the needs and demands of their powerful customers than they are to the demands, the interests or the privacy of their users, from whom they receive no revenue.

This business model makes it hard to identify effective legal or regulatory requirements for online service providers. Both those who sell and those who purchase the use of data gain access and influence: yet neither need be responsive to the interests or needs of the (non-paying) users whose data they collect, use and sell. Unsurprisingly, the recipients of targeted content may be unable to identify or assess the source of content they receive, or judge its accuracy, its truth or its trustworthiness. Socrates was right that communication is hard to assess or to hold to account if provenance is hidden.

Anonymity and Privacy

The claim that the anonymous exercise of power and influence is an underlying problem for online communication may seem surprising. Anonymity is often seen as closely linked to privacy, even as a matter of right. However, the right to privacy does not support a right to anonymity, since it protects only the limited range of content classified as 'personal' information (Chapter 6). In some cases, protecting personal information may (as it happens) secure anonymity, but this is not usually the case.

Some commentators have argued that if there is a right to privacy, there must also be a right to anonymity. For example, the respected press freedom organisation, Article 19, has argued that

The protection of anonymity is a vital component in protecting both the right to freedom of expression and the right to privacy. Anonymity allows individuals to express themselves without fear of reprisal, and is especially important in those countries where freedom of expression is heavily censored. It enables whistle-blowers to come forward and individuals to disclose their innermost concerns on a variety of issues in internet chat rooms. It also allows users simply to join in with all manner of discussions that they might otherwise avoid.[16]

This line of thought is unconvincing. There are indeed cases where anonymity is needed for ethically important reasons – whistle-blowers and investigative journalists are the standard examples. There are also cases where anonymity is not needed, but is unlikely to damage, for example where authors or benefactors choose anonymity. But there is no right to anonymity for those who protect or disguise ethically unacceptable or unlawful action. The anonymity often enjoyed by those who organise or purchase online influence is not a matter of right, and is not protected by the right to privacy. Ethically and epistemically unacceptable communication, such as spreading false information and accusations, corrupting democratic process, defaming others or spying on them, promoting illegal activities or false advertising, inciting violence or hatred, should not be protected.

There is a narrow case for protecting anonymity for investigative journalists who risk their freedom – or more – by speaking truth to power in and about oppressive states or illegal activity. Privacy, by contrast, is not a right only for those doing admirable but dangerous things. It is a right for everyone. However, it is a narrow right to one's '*privacy, family, home or correspondence*', and not a right to deceive, defraud, defame or misrepresent others anonymously.

Anonymity and Democracy

In many areas of life, and especially of public life, anonymity has long been seen as damaging or unacceptable, and there is no case for protecting it. Public activities need to take place 'in the public sphere', and should allow others to obtain relevant information, to witness, to assess, and to respond in various ways. Covert communication is often inadequate, and incompatible with democracy. Famously, Woodrow Wilson expanded this standard point rather too far when he argued that diplomatic negotiations should be a matter of

> Open covenants of peace, openly arrived at, after which there shall be no private international understandings of any kind but diplomacy shall proceed always frankly and in the public view.[17]

But while this may demand too much of diplomatic (or commercial) negotiations, it is an important standard for the outcomes of such negotiations in democracies. Scientific inquiry too requires honest and open communication about the methods used and the results achieved. Anonymous and unaccountable communication can damage democracy and science, public life and culture, and other public communication.

It is unsurprising that digital technologies, which ten years ago were seen as enabling and spreading democracy, are now widely seen as undermining democratic process. But the thought that connectivity would be enough for democracy was, in truth, never plausible, and depended on a selective and trivialising view of democracy. Democracy needs far more than free and fair elections and universal suffrage. It also requires governance that secures *order, the rule of law*, some version of the *separation of powers*, as well as at least some *human rights*. Without these, the possibility of well-functioning democratic politics recedes, and democracy may be reduced to mob rule – as Plato pointed out. Without *order*, there could be anarchy, and no reliable possibility of democratic governance. Without the *rule of law*, order could reflect the will of whoever is in power, and could be erratic, unpredictable, and incompatible with democratic public life. Without some form of the *separation of powers*, power could be dangerously concentrated, and might not support democratic governance in the longer run. Even with order, the rule of law and some version of the separation of powers, but without at least the *elementary rights of the person*, a regime that relied on elections might not provide stable democratic governance. Indeed, without the right electoral processes democracy can be damaged by elections themselves, including by some forms of digital campaigning.[18] Many regimes that provide order and the rule of law concentrate too much power in certain individuals, institutions or office holders, or impose harsh or unjust laws that do not respect the elementary rights of the person. Any democracy worth having demands far more than a universal franchise and periodic elections, and there are many reasons why connectivity is not enough for democracy.

Intermediaries Again: Old and New

The familiar intermediaries that disciplined communication in the pre-digital era – editors, printers, publishers, translators, librarians and many others – were tasked with ensuring that communication met certain ethical and epistemic standards. The new intermediaries – including online service providers, social media companies, data brokers, advertising agencies, influencers and some of their powerful customers – between them control and organise the provision, marketing and use of a large range of digital content, yet may not face comparable requirements.

The breaches of ethical and epistemic standards that then arise are likely to reflect the aims and organisation of digital service providers and can be at the expense of originators, of recipients, or of both. Originators may find their privacy breached: their views, appearance, personal information or location may become known to others whom they did not wish to become aware of them, or they may be misrepresented or maligned. Recipients may receive not only unwanted content – a nuisance, but not usually damaging – but misinformation or disinformation that has been selected to seem plausible and to influence them, or defamatory content and misinformation about others. They may also find it harder to identify reliable information. These deficiencies can damage democratic governance, poison cultural life and corrupt scientific research and communication.

Who benefits from these types of (mis)communication and these ways of limiting accountability for the content communicated? Beneficiaries no doubt include those who organise and sell online services or organise and market advertising, whose ability to shape others' beliefs and preferences may be enhanced if they can do so anonymously. They also include those who commission and fund the targeted distribution of selective information, misinformation and disinformation, of persuasion and influence. In the digital age propaganda campaigns no longer require state action: they are now commodities that can be purchased, and some of those who devise, market and pay for them are protected by anonymity.[19]

Unsurprisingly, then, recipients can find it hard to identify who has paid for and shaped – or distorted – the digital communication they receive. When print and radio, film and television, were the dominant technologies for wider communication, readers, listeners and viewers could be reasonably sure that they received the same content as others: what was provided was in that sense *public* information, and the question to be addressed was whether it was correct. Moreover, the legislation surrounding older communication technologies allowed readers, listeners and viewers who were misrepresented or misinformed to identify originators and to seek redress for speech wrongs, such as breach of intellectual property rights, fraud or defamation, misinformation or misrepresentation, including false reporting. Rectification and redress were in principle feasible, although often costly or hard to pursue. The old intermediaries were imperfect, and sometimes prevented, damaged or distorted communication, even in democratic states. However, many of them supported communication that met at least a range of ethical and epistemic standards. And since they were not anonymous, they could in principle be held to account and criticised for failings.

The new intermediaries *appear* more benign. But their power is not disciplined in analogous ways, and (despite much discussion), there is so far little effective legislation and regulation to protect those who are misrepresented, misinformed or misled by communication that uses digital technologies. The new intermediaries include not only the large tech companies, but other service providers, data brokers, advertising agencies, data storage companies, as well as their frequently anonymous customers, who purchase (the use of) personal data in order to wield influence without accountability.[20] These new intermediaries make money by organising data obtained from users of online technologies in order to target those whom they variously seek to inform or misinform, to influence or to persuade. Unsurprisingly, it can be hard or impossible for those whose data are traded to tell who is holding or using their data or what it is being used for, and difficult or even impossible to tell who is controlling – or perhaps inventing – the political or commercial content that is communicated. It is not hard to describe some of the risks: but identifying risks is not enough to identify remedies.

Platforms and Publishers

One repeatedly discussed and tempting proposal for making online communication and services more accountable takes the bull by the horns. It proposes that providers of digital services be treated in law as publishers, putting them on a par with print and broadcast media. This sounds simple and sensible, yet may be neither feasible nor sufficient.

There are two quite separate reasons why requiring the providers of digital services to take on the responsibilities of publishers may not provide a remedy. The first is that it is often not feasible for organisations that provide platforms on which others post content to subject all the content posted to prior scrutiny of the sort that publishers of print or broadcast material are required to provide. Publishers who fail to provide that scrutiny can be held to account for publishing material that they should not have published, for example because others hold the copyright, or because it is defamatory, or because it does not meet other ethical or epistemic standards. Platforms, however, may host so much content that prior scrutiny is not feasible. And while relying on subsequent scrutiny, followed by labelling or taking down unacceptable content, may be feasible, this allows interested parties to be the arbiters of acceptable speech.

Some commentators maintain that this difficulty is readily overcome. The wrong and damage that can be produced by online distribution of various sorts of content are, they suggest, a sufficient reason to take the bull by the horns and regulate providers of online services as publishers. For example, Roger Kay writes, with some sarcasm:

> So, Facebook, Google, and Twitter would have a hard time finding enough real editors to maintain their current scale. And that's the point, isn't it? They shouldn't have that scale, which comes from a distortion

of the click-based advertising model. Left to a more
"circulation" based model – where people pay for that
they get – scale wouldn't be such a critical issue.

Make the platforms responsible for 100% of the
content on their pages, and they would rapidly find a way
to ensure they weren't violating the law, which would
lead to a whole lot less – but better – material.

While old media like the *New York Times* remain
publishers, responsible for what appears in their pages,
the platforms are sticking to the story that they're just
"common carriers," like the phone companies.[21]

However, while this switch might be desirable and deserved,
it may not be achievable. Kay's suggestion not merely
demands that online service providers be treated and regulated as publishers, and held responsible for material on
their platforms. It demands that their entire business model
be re-engineered by regulating and limiting users' freedom
to post as they choose.

Publishers and providers of online services have
quite different relationships with their respective customers.
Publishers generally have many customers, some with little
interest in remaining anonymous. They may include book-
shops and newsagents, schools and universities, as well as
businesses and individual customers. Online service providers also have a range of customers who are not their
users and some of whom will have reasons to remain
anonymous. Those who purchase data in order to market
goods and services often need and seek to be identifiable, but
those who purchase them in order to sell ideologies and
disinformation, or to spread conspiracies and political

polarisation, do not. Customers who want to target specific audiences – whether to promote a particular cause or ideology, to swing an election or to damage a rival company or a foreign country – gain advantage if they can do so anonymously, or can recruit others to join political movements without their membership being a matter of public record.[22]

Limiting Anonymity, Extending Accountability

Anonymity does not always disrupt accountability. No harm is done if those with little power to harm or wrong others remain anonymous. But there is little case for allowing powerful and influential actors, including those who purchase (the use of) others' data in order to target and influence them, to benefit from anonymity. However, it does not follow that decisions to remove anonymity should be made by service providers.

Recent excursions into editorial terrain by some service providers illustrate the point.[23] Twitter's decision to close down former president Trump's account was controversial, even in the eyes of many who did not share or admire the president's politics. The excessive power and influence that some providers of online services already exercise cannot be curbed by providing them with additional powers to control others' communication.

However, removing anonymity from the powerful vendors, organisers and purchasers of targeted content is compatible with protecting privacy for individual users of online services. Removing anonymity from the powerful is necessary if their activities are to be regulated. It is a first – and only a first – step towards accountability. Only if those who control, fund and influence the targeting of digital communication can be identified, can they be held to account. Making them identifiable opens the gate to legislation and regulation that require them to support honest and accurate communication, and to respect further ethical and epistemic standards. The legislation and regulation to which they would be subject need not mirror that which applies to publishers in all respects, but many of the aims need to be the same. And once there are incentives for communication to meet ethical and epistemic standards, it becomes possible to organise ways of seeking redress for damage or injury done by communication that fails to do so.

Reshaping accountability to protect ethical and epistemic standards for communication will not be simple. If anonymity is to be removed from the powerful, while respecting individuals' rights to privacy, it will be necessary to distinguish cases with care. This suggests that the first step must be to determine which organisers of digital campaigns and which of their customers require regulating, and which do not raise problems (for example because they are too small, already regulated by other measures, or are not anonymous). Removing anonymity from powerful players and intermediaries will not, of course, be enough to discipline digital communication. But it is a necessary first step towards ensuring that the powerful can be held to account for respecting ethical and epistemic standards for digital communication.

NOTES

Preface

1 See Chapters 5 and 6.

Chapter 1

1 C. A. J. Coady, *Testimony: A Philosophical Study* (Oxford University Press, 1992).

2 Quassim Cassam, *Conspiracy Theories* (Cambridge: Polity Press, 2019); Ben Sasse (Senator for Nebraska), 'QAnon is Destroying the Republican Party from Within', *The Atlantic*, 16 January 2021, www.theatlantic.com/ideas/archive/2021/01/conspiracy-theories-will-doom-republican-party/617707. See also Chapter 7.

3 See Chapter 3.

4 Roger Brownsword, *Law, Technology and Society: Re-Imagining the Regulatory Environment* (Abingdon: Routledge, 2019), p. 7. For discussion of differences between technological and normative approaches to regulation see pp. 6–10.

5 For an argument that online payment systems should be seen not merely as a form of communication but as media, see Lana Swartz, *New Money: How Payment Became Social Media* (New Haven, Conn.: Yale University Press, 2020).

6 James Williams, *Stand Out of Our Light: Freedom and Resistance in the Attention Economy* (Cambridge University Press, 2018), p. 87.

7 *Ibid.*

8 Norbert Wiener, *Cybernetics: Or Control and Communication in the Animal and the Machine* (Paris: Hermann; Cambridge, Mass.: MIT Press, 1948; 2nd edn 1961), esp. p. 11. The term derives from the Greek word for *governing* or *steering*, so is apt for uses of digital technologies to control processes. For current examples, see the reports of the Oxford Computational Project at https://comprop.oii.ox.ac.uk/tag/cyber-troops.

Chapter 2

1 Older practices of surveillance were already highly intrusive. See for example the descriptions of Stasi practice in former East Germany in Uwe Johnson's chilling *Mutmassungen über Jakob* (Frankfurt: Suhrkamp, 1959), and in Timothy Garton Ash, *The File: A Personal History* (London: HarperCollins, 1997).

2 For recent accounts of surveillance using digital technologies, see Bruce Schneier, *Data and Goliath: The Hidden Battles to Collect Your Data and Control Your World* (New York: W. W. Norton, 2015), and Shoshana Zuboff, *The Age of Surveillance Capitalism: The Fight for a Human Future at the New Frontier of Power* (London: Profile, 2019).

3 Robert Darnton, *The Forbidden Bestsellers of Pre-Revolutionary France* (New York: W. W. Norton, 1996).

4 In the UK the *Online Harms White Paper* (April 2019, CP 57), has been subject to public consultation, and government response, but legislation has not been enacted. See *Online Harms White Paper: Full Government Response to the Consultation* (December 2020, CP 354). The central proposal is that online activity should be subject to a *duty of care*. This has been summarised as follows: 'The idea of a "duty of care" is straightforward in principle. A person (including companies) under a duty of care must take care in relation to a particular

116

activity as it affects particular people or things. If that person does not take care and someone comes to harm as a result then there are legal consequences. A duty of care does not require a perfect record – the question is whether sufficient care has been taken' (William M. Perrin, Lorna Woods and Maeve Walsh, *The Online Harms White Paper: A Summary Response from the Carnegie UK Trust*, June 2019, www.carnegieuktrust .org.uk/blog/online-harms-response-cukt). This approach avoids any need to predict that certain speech acts will actually inflict harm.

5 See Chapter 7 for further comment on these events.

6 Further discussion in Chapters 5 and 6.

7 Zuboff, *Age of Surveillance Capitalism.*

8 Samantha Bradshaw and Philip N. Howard, *The Global Disinformation Disorder: 2019 Global Inventory of Organised Social Media Manipulation.* Oxford Internet Institute, Working Paper 2019.2.

Chapter 3

1 Rory Stewart, 'Lord of Misrule', review of Tom Bower, *Boris Johnson: The Gambler*, W. H. Allen, in *Times Literary Supplement,* 6 November 2020, www.the-tls.co.uk/articles/ boris-johnson-tom-bower-book-review-rory-stewart. Stewart was Minister of State in the Foreign Office when an MP, and was sacked by the then Foreign Secretary, Boris Johnson. See Chapters 5 and 6.

2 The topic is large and currently much discussed. See, for example, Adam Etinson (ed.), *Human Rights: Moral or Political* (Oxford University Press, 2018); Nigel Biggar *What's Wrong with Rights?* (Oxford University Press, 2020).

3 Exodus 20:2–17 and *Deuteronomy* 5:6–21. King James translation. (Numbering varies since several passages of Scripture are relevant.)

4 See Chapters 5 and 6.

5 Plato, *Phaedrus*, 275d–e, trans. W. Hamilton (Harmondsworth: Penguin, 1973). For a classical treatment of differences between speech and writing, see Walter Ong, *Orality and Literacy: The Technologizing of the Word* (London: Methuen, 1982; reissued by Routledge in 2012), esp. pp. 78ff., where Ong explicitly compares the introduction of writing with that of computers.

6 Gutenberg's printed Bible appeared in the 1450s. Copyright was legally defined and enforced only with the passage of the Statute of Anne in 1710, and internationally protected only from the late nineteenth century.

7 This can happen in democratic as well as autocratic states. For example, the capture of parts of the print media by corporate and related interests was evident in the UK during the first years of the twenty-first century, leading up to the Leveson Inquiry in 2011; see Brian Leveson, *An Inquiry into the Culture, Practices and Ethics of the Press*, 3 vols. (London: Stationery Office, 2012), vol. 1. The then prime minister, Tony Blair, referred to parts of the print media at that time as 'feral media', and this phrase was widely quoted. See the essays reprinted in 'Tony Blair's "Media" Speech: The Commentators', *Political Quarterly*, 78/4 (2007), 476–87.

8 See Chapter 7.

9 See Jamie Bartlett, *The People vs Tech: How the Internet Is Killing Democracy (and How We Save It)* (London: Ebury Press, 2018); Carole Cadwalladr, 'Facebook's Role in Brexit – and the Threat to Democracy', TED Talk, 2019; Samantha Bradshaw and Philip N. Howard, 'Contentious Narratives: Digital Technology and the Attack on Liberal Democratic Norms', *Journal of International Affairs*, 71 (2018), 22–32; see also Chapter 7.

10 See Leveson, *Inquiry*.

11 Martin Gurri, *The Revolt of the Public and the Crisis of Authority in the New Millennium* (San Francisco, Calif.: Stripe Press, 2018).

12 See Chapter 7 for further discussion.

13 For detailed discussion of the diversity of platforms and what they provide, see José van Dijck, Thomas Poell and Martijn de Waal, *The Platform Society: Public Values in a Connective World* (Oxford University Press, 2018); and José van Dijck, *The Culture of Connectivity: A Critical History of Social Media* (New York: Oxford University Press, 2013). See also Chapter 7.

14 See, for example, Franklin Foer, *World without Mind: The Existential Threat of Big Tech* (London: Jonathan Cape, 2017); Alan Rusbridger, *Breaking News: The Remaking of Journalism and Why It Matters Now* (Edinburgh: Canongate, 2018); Martin Moore, *Democracy Hacked: Political Turmoil and Information Warfare in the Digital Age* (London: Bloomsbury, 2018); Bartlett, *The People vs. Tech*; James Williams, *Stand Out of Our Light: Freedom and Resistance in the Attention Economy* (Cambridge University Press, 2018); Mediatique, *Overview of Recent Dynamics in the UK Press Market* (London: Department for Digital, Culture, Media and Sport, 2018), https://assets.publishing.service .gov.uk/government/uploads/system/uploads/attachment_data/ file/720400/180621_Mediatique_-_Overview_of_recent_ dynamics_in_the_UK_press_market_-_Report_for_DCMS.pdf.

15 See Chapters 6 and 7.

Chapter 4

1 For remarkably early misgivings, see Todd Gitlin, *Media Unlimited: How the Torrent of Images and Sounds Overwhelms Our Lives* (London: Picador, 2002; rev. edn 2007).

2 The comment was in an interview in which he argued that anti-trust measures do not offer the right remedy for the problems that have arisen. Widely reported, including in the *New York Times*, 21 October 2020. For limited comments on anti-trust remedies to these problems, see Chapter 7.

3 See Martin Gurri, *The Revolt of the Public and the Crisis of Authority in the New Millennium* (San Francisco, Calif.: Stripe Press, 2018). See also Chapter 7.

4 See, for example, Quassim Cassam, *Conspiracy Theories* (Cambridge: Polity Press, 2019).

5 Books and films about censorship and control of pre-digital communication under twentieth-century totalitarian regimes have illustrated these points in excruciating detail. For discussions of practices in the former Soviet Union, see Aleksandr Solzhenitsyn, *The Gulag Archipelago: An Experiment in Literary Investigation* (1973); Nadezhda Mandelstam, *Hope against Hope* (1970). For discussions of the practices in former East Germany, see Uwe Johnson, *Mutmassungen über Jakob* (Frankfurt: Suhrkamp, 1959); Timothy Garton Ash, *The File: A Personal History* (London: HarperCollins, 1997); Florian Henckel von Donnersmarck's 2006 film *Das Leben der Anderen* (*The Lives of Others*). The list is depressingly large.

6 See Jonathan Taplin, *Move Fast and Break Things: How Facebook, Google and Amazon Cornered Culture and Undermined Democracy* (London: Pan, 2018). For robustly critical views see also Roger McNamee, *Zucked: Waking Up to the Facebook Catastrophe* (London: HarperCollins, 2019); Shoshana Zuboff, *The Age of Surveillance Capitalism: The Fight for a Human Future at the New Frontier of Power* (London: Profile, 2019); Jamie Bartlett, *The People vs Tech,* Penguin, 2018.

7 See Alan Rusbridger, *Breaking News: The Remaking of Journalism and Why It Matters Now* (Edinburgh: Canongate,

2018), and Martin Moore, *Democracy Hacked: Political Turmoil and Information Warfare in the Digital Age* (London: Bloomsbury, 2018), for accounts of the effect of digital technologies on traditional, including public interest, journalism.

8 See Tim Berners-Lee, 'One Small Step for the Web', 23 October 2018, https://inrupt.com/blog/one-small-step-for-the-web. He has since launched *The Contract for the Web*, described as 'an initiative to bring governments, companies, and civil society and web users together to build a roadmap for how we build a web that serves humanity and is a public good for everyone, everywhere'. See also https://webfoundation.org/2019/03/web-birthday-30/

9 See Rusbridger, *Breaking News.*

10 For evidence on journalism, see *The Cairncross Review: A Sustainable Future for Journalism*, 12 February 2019, https://assets.publishing.service.gov.uk/government/uploads/system/uploads/attachment_data/file/779882/021919_DCMS_Cairncross_Review_.pdf. For evidence on the effects of digital technologies on musicians and writers, see Taplin, *Move Fast and Break Things*; for evidence on professional writers' earnings, see the website of the Authors' Licensing and Collecting Society. For discussion of some traditional intermediaries, see Franklin Foer, *World without Mind: The Existential Threat of Big Tech* (London: Jonathan Cape, 2017); Rusbridger, *Breaking News*; and Moore, *Democracy Hacked.*

11 Cf. Albert Weale, *The Will of the People* (Cambridge: Polity Press, 2018).

12 See Foer, *World without Mind*; Rusbridger, *Breaking News*; Stephen Levitsky and Daniel Ziblatt, *How Democracies Die: What History Reveals about Our Future* (London: Penguin, 2018).

Chapter 5

1 Horace, *Odes*, III.2.13.

2 Wilfred Owen, 'Dulce et Decorum est' (first published 1921) in *Wilfred Owen: The War Poems*, ed. Jon Stallworthy (London: Chatto & Windus, 1994).

3 Subjective views of ethics consider each person's 'values' – the principles they happen to hold – as justification for action. This conceit was nicely lampooned in the 1930s (it is said by Groucho Marx) with the comment 'Yes, I have principles, and if you do not like them I have some others.'

4 The status of appeals to human rights is controversial. Doubts whether human rights have a moral justification and claims that their authority derives from the fact that states have promulgated them are currently hotly disputed. See Samuel Moyn, *The Last Utopia: Human Rights in History* (Cambridge, Mass.: Harvard University Press, 2010); Stephen Hopgood, *The Endtimes of Human Rights* (Ithaca, NY: Cornell University Press, 2013); Eric Posner *The Twilight of Human Rights Law* (Oxford University Press, 2014); Noel Malcolm, *Human Rights and Political Wrongs: A New Approach to Human Rights Law* (Cambridge: Polity Press, 2018); Adam Etinson (ed.), *Human Rights: Moral or Political* (Oxford University Press, 2018); Nigel Biggar, *What's Wrong with Rights?* (Oxford University Press, 2020).

5 The disputed question is whether human rights can be supported by ethical justifications, or are positive rights instituted by the states party to the basic Declarations and Charters. For discussion, see the works cited in note 4.

6 Cf. Geert Van Eekert, 'Freedom of Speech, Freedom of Self-Expression, and Kant's Public Use of Reason', *Diametros* 54 (2018), 118–37.

7 *ECHR* Article 9 reads 'Everyone has the right to freedom of thought, conscience and religion; this right includes freedom to change his religion or belief and freedom, either alone or in

community with others and in public or private, to manifest his religion or belief, in worship, teaching, practice and observance.' Cf. *UDHR* Article 18.

8 John Stuart Mill, *On Liberty* (London: Penguin, 2010), 2.

9 *Ibid.*

10 Would Mill have thought that expressing this opinion on Twitter was acceptable? Or would he have concluded that the size of the potential audience made it more like voicing an opinion outside the house of the corn-dealer? See Chapter 7 for a contemporary view on this point.

11 *Schenck* v. *United States*, 249 US 47 (1919).

12 See Chapter 2.

13 See discussion of online harms in Chapter 2.

14 Bernard Williams, *Truth and Truthfulness: An Essay in Genealogy* (Princeton University Press, 2002), 217.

15 See, for example, the World Medical Association's *Declaration of Helsinki* whose successive versions set out principles for the conduct of medical research affecting human subjects in ever greater detail. www.wma.net/policies-post/wma-declaration-of-helsinki-ethical-principles-for-medical-research-involving-human-subjects.

16 See Chapters 4 and 7.

17 For recent discussions of some of the pressures on democracy in the digital age, see Albert Weale, *The Will of the People* (Cambridge: Polity Press, 2018); David Runciman, *How Democracy Ends* (London: Profile, 2018); Anne Applebaum, *The Twilight of Democracy: The Seductive Lure of Authoritarianism* (New York: Doubleday, 2020).

Chapter 6

1 See, for example, Bruce Schneier, *Data and Goliath: The Hidden Battles to Collect Your Data and Control Your World* (New York: W. W. Norton, 2015); Shoshana Zuboff , *The Age of*

Surveillance Capitalism: The Fight for a Human Future at the New Frontier of Power (London: Profile, 2019); Carissa Véliz, *Privacy Is Power: Why and How You Should Take Back Control of your Data* (London: Penguin, 2021).

2 Discussions of rights to privacy predate data protection approaches. For a classical paper, see S. Warren and L. Brandeis, 'The Right to Privacy', *Harvard Law Review*, 4 (1890), 193–220. For philosophical discussion of rights to privacy that predates digital technologies, see Judith Jarvis Thomson, 'The Right to Privacy', *Philosophy and Public Affairs*, 4 (1975), 295–314; and James Rachels, 'Why Privacy Is Important', *Philosophyand Public Affairs*, 4 (1975), 323–33.

3 For more detail on the possibilities, see Schneier, *Data and Goliath*; and Vélez, *Privacy Is Power*.

4 There are cases in which anonymity rather than privacy matters. They are different, and I shall comment on anonymity in the next chapter.

5 See Vélez, *Privacy Is Power*.

6 See 'Data Protection Act 1998: Legal Guidance', p. 15, https://content.next.westlaw.com/2-200-4571?__lrTS=20210629123410796&transitionType=Default&contextData=%28sc.Default%29.

7 Data Protection Act 1998, Part I, Section 1. This formulation is closely based on that of the European Directive 95/46/EC which states that '"personal data" shall mean any information relating to an identified or identifiable natural person ("data subject")' (Chapter 1, Article 2 (a)).

8 Some will think that the dead too are owed a measure of privacy. Cf. Geoffrey Scarre, 'Privacy and the Dead', *Philosophy in the Contemporary World*, 19/1 (2013), 1–16.

9 Information Commissioner's Office (ICO), https://ico.org.uk.

10 For long-standing definitions of *identifiable data* and of *reasonably identifiable data*, see Department of Health,

Confidentiality: NHS Code of Practice (2003), p. 9, www.dh.gov
.uk/assetRoot/04/06/92/54/04069254.pdf.

11 *New York Times*, 2 February 2019, www.nytimes.com/2019/02/
02/opinion/internet-facebook-google-consent.html. For the
hollowing out of consent requirements in biomedicine, see Neil
C. Manson and Onora O'Neill, *Rethinking Informed Consent in
Bioethics* (Cambridge University Press, 2007); Onora O'Neill,
'Humanity and Hyper-Regulation: From Nuremberg to
Helsinki' in *Ethics and Humanity: Themes from the Philosophy
of Jonathan Glover*, ed. Jeff McMahan, N. Ann Davis and
Richard Keshen (New York: Oxford University Press, 2009).

12 Paul R. Burton et. al., 'Data Safe Havens in Health Research
and Healthcare', *Bioinformatics*, 31/20 (October 2015), 3241–8,
https://doi.org/10.1093/bioinformatics/btv279. See also
Academy of Medical Sciences, *Data in Safe Havens*, March
2014, https://acmedsci.ac.uk/policy/policy-projects/data-in-
safe-havens. In effect safe havens bolt confidentiality
requirements onto data protection requirements, so do not rely
entirely on distinguishing personal from non-personal content.

Chapter 7

1 To appreciate how complex, see José van Dijck, *The Culture of
Connectivity: A Critical History of Social Media* (New York:
Oxford University Press, 2013); and José van Dijck, Thomas
Poell and Martijn de Waal *The Platform Society: Public Values
in a Connective World* (Oxford University Press, 2018).

2 For recent reports on the effects of digital communication on
democracy, see Forum on Information & Democracy, *Policy
Framework* (2020), https://informationdemocracy.org/wp-
content/uploads/2020/11/ForumID_Report-on-infodemics_
101120.pdf; Yochai Benkler, Robert Faris and Hal Roberts,
Network Propaganda: Manipulation, Disinformation, and

Radicalization in American Politics (New York: Oxford University Press, 2018); Kofi Annan Foundation, *Protecting Electoral Integrity in the Digital Age* (2020), www .kofiannanfoundation.org/app/uploads/2020/05/85ef4e5d-kaf-kacedda-report_2020_english.pdf; Electoral Reform Society, *Democracy in the Dark: Digital Campaigning in the 2019 General Election and Beyond* (2020), www.electoral-reform.org.uk/latest-news-and-research/publications/democracy-in-the-dark-digital-campaigning-in-the-2019-general-election-and-beyond; and the EU Commission's *European Democracy Action Plan* (2020), https://ec.europa.eu/commission/presscorner/detail/en/ip_20_2250 – and many, many other analyses.

3 Widely quoted on 28 May 2020, from the *Guardian* to *Fox News*. Editors do not generally see themselves as 'arbiters of truth' and the use of this phrase reveals a distinctive view of editing.

4 For immediate comments on deplatforming, see Anna Wiener, 'Trump's Been Unplugged. Now What?', *New Yorker*, 13 January 2021, www.newyorker.com/tech/annals-of-technology/big-tech-unplugs-trump.

5 On 24 February 2021, *The New York Times* commented: 'The action underscores the difficulties Facebook faces over what it allows on its site. Mark Zuckerberg, Facebook's chief executive, has long championed freedom of speech above all else, positioning the site as merely a platform and technology service that would not get involved in governmental or social disputes.'

6 The decision was widely criticised as an unacceptable breach of rights to freedom of expression, not only by libertarians but (for example) by Chancellor Merkel, by the French finance minister Bruno Le Maire, and by the Russian dissident Alexei

Navalny (presumably for differing reasons). See *Financial Times*, 11 January 2021.

7 Gilad Edelman, 'The Smoking Gun in the Facebook Antitrust Case', *Wired*, 9 December 2020: 'The company's journey from privacy focused start-up to mass surveillance platform is at the heart of the long-awaited antitrust case . . .'

8 Michael Latzer and Natascha Just, 'Governance by and of Algorithms on the Internet: Impact and Consequences' in *Oxford Research Encyclopedia of Communication*, ed. Jon F. Nussbaum (New York: Oxford University Press, 2014–); 'Algorithms Behaving Badly: 2020 Edition', *The Markup*, 15 December 2020, https://themarkup.org/2020-in-review/2020/12/15/algorithms-bias-racism-surveillance.

9 For details see https://gdpr.eu/right-to-be-forgotten.

10 For example, by keeping a record of the sorts of content recipients have already encountered – and in particular what they have 'liked' – and directing them to more . . . and more . . . of the same. See Gillian Tett, *The Silo Effect: The Peril of Expertise and the Promise of Breaking Down Barriers* (London: Little, Brown, 2015).

11 Prospective legislation in the UK is to include an Online Harms Bill. It is expected to require platforms to adopt a code of conduct setting out their responsibilities to children and to face fines if they fail to stick to them, and to bring online misinformation that is legal but could cause significant physical or psychological harm to adults under the remit of a regulator. Cf. Chapter 2.

12 Carissa Vélez, *Privacy Is Power: Why and How You Should Take Back Control of Your Data* (London: Penguin, 2021), p. 69.

13 However, digital technologies offer more versatile methods both for surveillance and for manipulating, influencing and controlling. See Shoshana Zuboff , *The Age of Surveillance Capitalism: The Fight for a Human Future at the New Frontier*

of Power (London: Profile, 2019); Bruce Schneier, *Data and Goliath: The Hidden Battles to Collect Your Data and Control Your World* (New York: W. W. Norton, 2015).

14 See Chapters 4 and 5.

15 As noted above, the polite fiction that service users consent to the reuse or sale of their personal data is undermined by the fact that online consent procedures – even to complex content – often require only 'tick and click' consent, rather than genuine consent.

16 Article 19, *The Right to Online Anonymity*, 18 June 2015.

17 Woodrow Wilson enunciated the fourteen points to Congress in January 1918.

18 Lisa-Maria Neudert, 'Hurdles and Pathways to Regulatory Innovation in Digital Political Campaigning', *Political Quarterly*, 91 (2020), 713–21, https://doi.org/10.1111/1467-923X .12915.

19 Piotr Pomerantsev, *This Is Not Propaganda: Adventures in the War against Reality* (London: Faber and Faber, 2019).

20 The detail is varied and complicated. Cf. Schneier, *Data and Goliath*; Zuboff, *Age of Surveillance Capitalism*; van Dijck, *Culture of Connectivity*.

21 Roger Kay, 'Platform or Publisher?', *Medium*, 5 December 2019, https://medium.com/swlh/platform-or-publisher-f20f72f832b6; see also Vélez, *Privacy Is Power*.

22 Examples include voter deterrence campaigns, which try to persuade selected voters that it would be pointless for them to vote, and campaigns (such as 'Stop the Steal') that peddle false or misleading political information in order to corrupt elections.

23 See the 'Turning Point' section of this chapter.

SOME SUGGESTIONS FOR FURTHER READING

This book is about the many ethical and epistemic norms and standards that matter for communication, including digital communication. Some of the suggestions discuss norms and standards that matter for all communication, whether or not it uses digital technologies. These include rights to freedom of expression and to privacy, norms of truthfulness and trustworthiness, of toleration and transparency, of accuracy and honesty, and many more. Other suggestions discuss ways in which norms and standards that matter for communication can be disrupted, or even undermined, when communication uses digital technologies, and some of the changes that are called for.

A. J. Austin, *How to Do Things with Words: The William James Lectures delivered at Harvard University in 1955*, ed. J. O. Urmson and Marina Sbisà (Oxford: Clarendon Press, 1962).

Quassim Cassam, *Conspiracy Theories* (Cambridge: Polity Press, 2019).

C. A. J. Coady, *Testimony: A Philosophical Study* (Oxford University Press, 1992).

José van Dijck, *The Culture of Connectivity: A Critical History of Social Media*, New York, Oxford University Press, 2013.

José van Dijck, Thomas Poell and Martijn de Waal, *The Platform Society: Public Values in a Connective World* (Oxford University Press, 2018).

Franklin Foer, *World without Mind: The Existential Threat of Big Tech* (London: Jonathan Cape, 2017).

Katherine Hawley, *Trust: A Very Short Introduction* (Oxford University Press, 2012).

David Heald and Christopher Hood (eds.), *Transparency: The Key to Better Governance?* (Oxford University Press, 2006).

Roger McNamee, *Zucked: Waking Up to the Facebook Catastrophe* (London: HarperCollins, 2019).

John Stuart Mill, *On Liberty* (London: Penguin, 2010).

Martin Moore, *Democracy Hacked: Political Turmoil and Information Warfare in the Digital Age* (London: Bloomsbury, 2018).

Onora O'Neill, *A Question of Trust*, The BBC Reith Lectures (Cambridge University Press, 2002).
   Speech Rights and Speech Wrongs (Assen: Koninklijke Van Gorcum, 2016).

Walter Ong, *Orality and Literacy: The Technologizing of the Word* (London: Methuen, 1982); reissued by Routledge in 2012.

Piotr Pomerantsev, *This Is Not Propaganda: Adventures in the War against Reality* (London: Faber and Faber, 2019).

James Rachels, 'Why Privacy Is Important', *Philosophy and Public Affairs*, 4 (1975), 323–33.

Alan Rusbridger, *Breaking News: The Remaking of Journalism and Why It Matters Now* (Edinburgh: Canongate, 2018).

T. M. Scanlon, *The Difficulty of Tolerance: Essays in Political Philosophy* (Cambridge University Press, 2003).

Bruce Schneier, *Data and Goliath: The Hidden Battles to Collect Your Data and Control Your World* (New York: W. W. Norton, 2015).

Jonathan Taplin, *Move Fast and Break Things: How Facebook, Google and Amazon Cornered Culture and Undermined Democracy* (London: Pan, 2018).

Gillian Tett, *The Silo Effect: The Peril of Expertise and the Promise of Breaking Down Barriers* (London: Little, Brown, 2015).

Judith Jarvis Thomson, 'The Right to Privacy', *Philosophy and Public Affairs*, 4 (1975), 295–314.

Carissa Véliz, *Privacy Is Power: Why and How You Should Take Back Control of your Data* (London, Penguin, 2021).

Jeremy Waldron and Melissa S. Williams (eds.), *Toleration and Its Limits* (New York: NYU Press, 2008).

S. Warren, and L. Brandeis, 'The Right to Privacy', *Harvard Law Review*, 4 (1890), 193–220.

Norbert Wiener, *Cybernetics: Or Control and Communication in the Animal and the Machine* (Paris: Hermann; Cambridge, Mass.: MIT Press, 1948; 2nd edn 1961).

Bernard Williams, *Truth and Truthfulness: An Essay in Genealogy* (Princeton University Press, 2002).

Shoshana Zuboff, *The Age of Surveillance Capitalism: The Fight for a Human Future at the New Frontier of Power* (London: Profile, 2019).

INDEX

academic freedom, 65–6
accessibility, 3–5, 46–52, 56. *See also*
    originators; recipients;
    technical norms
  definition, 4
  widening, 7–8
accountability, 109
  anonymity and, 98
  of corporate actors, 104
  of customers, 104
  digital technology and, 99–100
  extending, 114
  of originators, 101–2
  for speech content, 97–8
  of state actors, 104
  of users, 104
accuracy, 25, 29. *See* epistemic
    norms
advertisements, 102
  political, 40–1, 94–6
aesthetic norms, 25–6
Alexa, 78
algorithms, 9
ancient norms for communication,
    32–4
anonymity, 83–4, 87
  accountability and, 98
  democracy and, 107–8
  intermediaries and, 110

  limiting, 114
  privacy and, 105–6
  publishers and, 112–13
anti-trust measures, 94, 120
anti-vaccination movement, 98
Article 19, 104–5
Artificial Intelligence, 9
assessability, 4–5. *See also* technical
    norms
  recipients and, 53–4
attentiveness, 25
audibility, 25–6
autonomous vehicles, 9

Berners-Lee, Tim, 52
Bible
  Gutenberg, 118
  Ten commandments, 32–3
Blair, Tony, 118
Bower, Tom, 30–1
Brexit, 49
Brownsword, Roger, 9
bullying, 19, 29–30

Cambridge Analytica, 49
care, duty of, 116–17
censorship, 45–52, 120–1
  in China, 16–17
  Zuckerberg on, 92–3

cheating, 26, 29–30
China, censorship in, 16–17
civility, 24–5, 33–4
clarity, 25–6
Coady, Tony, 6
coherence, 25
commandments, Biblical, 32–3
communication rights, 24–5, 61–74
communication technologies, 12–13.
    See also digital technologies;
    printing; written word
comprehensibility, 25. *See also*
    intelligibility
confidentiality, 29–30
connectivity, 38–9, 44–7
    and democracy, 53, 107–8
    and digital technologies, 46–7
    and privacy rights, 77–8
consistency, 25, 29
conspiracy theories, 98
copyright, 118
corporations, accountability of, 104
corruption, 29
counterpart rights, duties with,
    24–5, 33–4, 61–4, 71. *See also*
    duties; imperfect duties;
    perfect duties
customers
    constrasted with users, 100–1
    lack of accountability, 104
cyber
    bullying, 13
    crime, 13
    intelligence, 13
    warfare, 13
cybernetics, 13

data
    ethics, 8–9
    harvesting, 78
    medical, 83–4, 87
    personal, 84–7, 94–6
Data Protection Directive, 80
deception, 29–30
Declaration of Helsinki, 84–5
defamation, 26, 29–30, 39
democracy, 45–52
    anonymity and, 107–8
    checks and balances in, 54–5
    connectivity and, 53, 107–8
    damage by digital technology,
        43, 52, 54–5
    freedom of expression in, 63–74
    intermediaries and, 53–6
deplatforming, 126
digital literacy, 94
digital platforms, fact-checking on,
    42–3
digital technologies. *See also*
    specific topics
    accountability and, 99–100
    change and, 11–12
    communication and, 7–8
    connectivity and, 46–7
    debate on, 22–3
    democracy damaged by, 43, 52,
        54–5
    information and
        misinformation disseminated
        by, 45–6
    optimism about, 44–52
    originators and, 7, 11–12, 57
    privacy and, 76–7

digital technologies. (cont.)
  recipients and, 7, 11–12, 44–52,
    57, 109–10
discretion, 25, 29–30, 33–4
dishonest speech acts, 20–1
disinformation, 18, 29–30
disintermediation, 54–6
Dorsey, Jack, 93–4
"Dulce et Decorum est" (Owen),
    61–2
duties
  of care, 116–17
  with counterpart rights, 24–5,
    33–4, 61–4, 71
  epistemic, 63
  history of, 61–4
  imperfect, 25, 62–3
  perfect, 24–5, 62–3

ECHR. See European Convention
    on Human Rights
elections, 40–1. See also democracy
elementary rights, 54–5, 107–8
epistemic
  duties, 63
  norms, 25, 29–30, 38–9, 53–4, 71
ethical norms, 24–5, 29–30, 38–9,
    53–4, 71
ethics of communication, 61. See
    also norms; standards
  and digital ethics, 8–9
  harms and, 17–19
  human rights and, 91
  norms and, 17–19
  open-endedness of, 31
  private harms and, 21

public harms and, 23–4
  speech acts and, 16–17
  speech content and, 16–17
euphemism, 16–17
European Convention on Human
    Rights (ECHR), 64–5, 75
  Article 9, 122–3
  Article 10, 66–7, 70–1
  and privacy, 75–6
evasion, 26
evidence, respect for, 25. See also
    epistemic norms
exaggeration, 26
expression. See freedom of
    expression

Facebook, 47, 51, 92–3, 111–12
fact-checking, 94–6
  on digital platforms, 42–3
falsity, 26
filter bubbles, 94–6
France, 16–17
fraud, 26, 29–30
free digital services, 103–4
free speech, 65–6
  as free expression, 68
  originators and, 65–6
  qualification of, 70–1
freedom of expression, 24–5, 33,
    50–1, 56
  circumstances and, 68–71
  communication and, 67–8
  in democracy, 63–74
  history of turn to, 64–7
  libertarianism and, 72–3
  political correctness and, 72–3

private harms and, 71–4
public harms and, 71–4
in scientific research, 73
freedom of information, 26, 44

General Regulation on Data
    Protection, 80
Google, 111–12
grammaticality, 25–6
Gutenberg Bible, 118

harmony, 25–6
harms
    definition, 17
    demonstrability of, 20–1
    in ethics of communication,
        17–19
    incidence of, 19–20
    lies causing, 21
    online, 18–19, 23–4,
        94–6
    originators causing, 17–18
    private, 21, 71–4
    public, 21–4, 71–4
    on social media, 18–19
    unintended, 20
Holmes, Oliver Wendell, 70
honesty, 29–30, 33–4
human rights, 61–74, 96–7, 107–8.
    See also European
    Convention on Human
    Rights; freedom of expression;
    privacy, rights to; Universal
    Declaration of Human Rights
    canonical documents on, 25,
        64–5, 70–1

in ethics of communication, 91
    standards, 32–3, 56

ICT. See information and
    communication technologies
imperfect duties, 62–3
    norms for, 25
imprints, 40, 48–9
influencers, 54
information and communication
    technologies (ICT), 12–13
information campaigning,
    26
Information Commissioner's
    Office, 82
information processing, 81
informed consent
    personal data and, 84–6
    procedures, 85, 128
intelligibility. See also technical
        norms
    of communication, 3–5
    definition, 4
    of language, 5–6
intermediaries, 39–40, 103. See also
        media; social media
    anonymity and, 110
    breaking of, 47–51
    and common carriers,
        112
    democracy and, 53–6
    new types of, 108–9
    regulation of, 110
    and state actors, 50
    traditional, 41–3, 50–5
Internet of things, 9

interpretation. *See* assessability; intelligibility; judgement
intimidation, 29–30

Johnson, Boris, 30–1
judgement. *See also* indeterminacy; interpretation
  proportionate resolution, 32
judiciary, 54–5

Kay, Roger, 111–12

language
  intelligibility of, 5–6
  translation of, 5–6
legacy media, 4–5
legibility, 25–6
Les Lettres Persanes (Montesquieu), 16
Leveson Inquiry, 118
libertarianism, 50–1, 63–74, 126
  on freedom of expression, 72–3
lies, 18, 26, 29–30
  harm caused by, 21
listeners, 41. *See also* originators; recipients
livres philosophiques, 16–17

machine learning, 9
malicious speech, 18, 21
manipulation, 29–30
McNamee, Roger, 51
media, social. *See* social media
media, traditional. *See* intermediaries; publishers
media capture, 118

medical data, 83–4, 87
Mill, John Stuart, 69, 123
moderation, 33–4
Montesquieu, 16
Move Fast and Break Things (Taplin), 51. *See also* Zuckerberg, Mark

norms, 20–1, 61. *See also* interpretation
  aesthetic, 25–6
  ancient, 32–4
  for communication, 24–7
  conflicts of, 31
  epistemic, 25, 29–30, 38–9, 53–4, 71
  ethical, 24–5, 29–30, 38–9, 53–4, 71
  in ethics of communication, 17–19
  for imperfect duties, 25
  justification of, 27
  for perfect duties, 24–5
  practical judgement and, 32
  for speech acts, 26
  system, 26
  technical, 25–6
Nuremberg Code, 84–5

online communication
  control of, 15–16
  regulation of, 94–6
online harms, 18–19, 23–4
  limiting, 94–6
Online Harms Bill, 127
openness, 33–4

originators, 4–5, 18, 28. *See also*
    recipients
    accountability of, 101–2
    digital technologies and, 7, 11–12,
        57
    free speech and, 65–6
    harms caused by, 17–18
    identification of, 28, 38–40, 42,
        48–9, 97–8, 109–10
    privacy rights of, 108–9
    protected rights of, 65–7
    recipient contact with, 35–7, 39,
        41
    respect for standards, 67–8
Owen, Wilfred, 61–2

Parler (site), 22–3
partisanship, 29, 38–9
patriotism, 62
perfect duties, 62–3
    norms for, 24–5
perjury, 26
personal data
    informed consent and, 84–6
    protection of, 87, 94–6
personal information, privacy
    rights and, 80–4
Phaedrus (Plato), 34–5
plagiarism, 26, 29–30, 39
platforms, 112–13
Plato, 34–5, 54–5
political advertising, 94–6
    regulation of, 40–1
populism, 63–74
practical judgement, 33
    indeterminacy of, 31

norms and, 32
    requirements, 31
press freedom, 65–6, 68
printing and publishing, 37–8
    regulation of, 39–40
privacy, rights to, 19, 24–5, 29–30,
        33, 56, 64–5, 75–8
    anonymity and, 105–6
    breach of, 26
    connectivity and, 77–8
    and digital technology, 76–7
    ECHR on, 75–6
    importance of, 79–80
    interferences with, 76–7
    of originators, 108–9
    personal information and, 80–4
    point of, 79–80
    in practice, 86–7
    recipients and, 79–80, 108–9
    UDHR on, 70–4
    Zuckerberg on, 78–9
private harms
    in ethics of communication, 21
    freedom of expression and, 71–4
propaganda, 29–30
provenance, 35, 40
public content, 101
public harms
    definition, 21–2
    in ethics of communication,
        23–4
    freedom of expression and, 71–4
publishers, 39, 42. *See also*
    intermediaries
    anonymity and, 112–13
    political freedom of, 68

QAnon, 98

readers, 41. *See also* listeners;
    recipients; viewers
recipients, 4–5, 28, 63–4, 97–8, 101.
    See also originators
  assessability and, 53–4
  digital technologies and, 7, 11–12,
    44–52, 57, 109–10
  identification of, 28
  originator contact with, 35–7, 39,
    41
  prioritizing, 66, 62–3
  privacy rights and, 79–80, 108–9
  protection of, 94–6
  respect for standards, 67–8
  rights of, 62–3
  targeted content, 104
referenda campaigns, 40–1
regulation
  by intermediaries, 110
  of political advertising, 40–1
  of printing, 39–40
religious freedom, 65–6
rights, 61–74. *See also* ethics of
    communication; human
    rights; privacy, rights to
  circumstances in cases
    involving, 68–71
  communication, 24–5, 61–74
  counterpart, 24–5, 33–4, 61–4,
    71
  before duties, 61–4
  elementary, 54–5, 107–8
  history of, 61–4
  of originators, 65–7

of recipients, 62–3
turn to, 64–7
rule of law, 54–5, 107–8

Schmidt, Eric, 44
scientific research, 23
  freedom of expression and
    communication in, 73
security, 33–4
self-expression, 65–6, 69
separation of powers, 54–5, 107–8
simplicity, 25–6
social media, 18, 44, 71, 102
  harms of, 18–19
  Trump and, 92–3
Socrates, 37, 97–8
speech acts
  dishonest, 20–1
  ethics of communication and,
    16–17
  norms for, 26
  offensive, 72–3
  requirements on, 15
  speech content distinct from,
    34–5
speech content. *See also* free speech
  accountability for, 97–8
  ethics of communication and,
    16–17
  prohibition of, 15–16
  speech acts different from, 34–5
  taboo speech, 15
spreading the word, 7–8
standards, 20–1, 61. *See also* norms
  for communication, 24–7
  conflicts of, 31

contextual differences for, 29
for digital technology, 63–74
human rights, 32–3, 56
justification of, 27
originator respect for, 67–8
recipient respect for, 67–8
state actors
accountability of, 104
Stewart, Rory, 30–1
surveillance, 26. *See also* privacy,
rights to
system
failings, 26
norms, 26

tact, 33–4
Taplin, Jonathan, 51–4
technical norms, 25–6
technology. *See also* digital
technology; intermediaries
communication and, 6–7, 12–13
written word as new, 37
The Republic (Plato), 54–5
tolerance, 33–4
totalitarianism, 50, 120–1
traditional intermediaries, 41–3, 50–5
translation, of language, 5–6
transparency, 26, 33–4
Trump, Donald, 22–3, 49, 54–5, 113
on social media, 92–3
trust, trustworthiness, 29–30, 33–4
truth, 17–18, 25, 71–2
Twitter, 92–3, 111–13

UDHR. *See* Universal Declaration
of Human Rights

unintended harms, 20
United Kingdom, 40–1
Universal Declaration of Human
Rights (UDHR), 75
Article 19, 64–5
on privacy rights, 70–4
US Capitol invasion, January 2021,
43, 92–3
users
accountability of, 104
distinct from customers, 100–1

values, 122
Vélez, Carisa, 98
viewers, 41. *See also* recipients
voter deterrence campaigns,
128

Wiener, Norbert, 13
Williams, Bernard, 71–2
Williams, James, 12–13
Wilson, Woodrow, 106
World War II, 62
written word
advantages of, 36
as new technology, 37
provenance of, 35
speech acts and content
separated by, 34–5

Zucked (McNamee), 51
Zuckerberg, Mark, 47–8, 50–1,
53
on censorship, 92–3
criticisms of, 51–2
on privacy rights, 78–9